AFTER THE BODY

CLEOPATRA MATHIS

After the Body

POEMS NEW AND SELECTED

SARABANDE BOOKS *Louisville, KY*

Library of Congress Cataloging-in-Publication Data

Names: Mathis, Cleopatra, 1947– author.
Title: After the body : poems new and selected / Cleopatra Mathis.
Description: First edition. | Louisville, Ky : Sarabande Books, 2020.
Identifiers: LCCN 2019032576 (print) | LCCN 2019032577 (e-book)
ISBN 9781946448606 (trade paperback) | ISBN 9781946448613 (e-book)
Subjects: LCSH: Human body—Poetry. | Control (Psychology)—Poetry.
Classification: LCC PS3563.A8363 A6 2020 (print)
LCC PS3563.A8363 (e-book) | DDC 811/.54—dc23
LC record available at https://lccn.loc.gov/2019032576
LC e-book record available at https://lccn.loc.gov/2019032577

Cover and interior design by Alban Fischer.
Manufactured in Canada.
This book is printed on acid-free paper.
Sarabande Books is a nonprofit literary organization.

This project is supported in part by an award from the National Endowment for the Arts.
The Kentucky Arts Council, the state arts agency, supports Sarabande Books with state
tax dollars and federal funding from the National Endowment for the Arts.

CONTENTS

NEW POEMS

This Time, the Hawk / 1

The Difference / 2

Bed-Bound / 3

After Chemo / 4

Not Myself / 5

Dyskinesia / 6

Through the Coffin Window / 7

Mother Pain / 9

The News at Two A.M. / 10

Arm, Etc. / 11

What the Knife Is For / 13

Mother / 14

Spring / 15

Unfinished / 16

The Year / 18

The River / 19

Going Under / 21

Broke / 22

The Old Self / 23

The Body, Full of Bias / 24

Being Apart / 26

After the Body / 27

Silver / 28

SELECTED POEMS

from *Aerial View of Louisiana* (1979)
Aerial View of Louisiana / 33
For Maria / 34
As You Stalk the Sleep of My Forgetting / 35
A Place of Another Name / 37
Bees / 39
Getting Out / 40
Padre Island / 41

from *The Bottom Land* (1983)
Black Walnut / 45
For Blue / 46
Body, Earth, Water / 48
Elegy for the Other / 50
White Field / 58
On the Twelfth of March / 59
Fort Wall at Mytilene: Greece, 1921 / 60
Moon and Stars over Crete: For Alexandra / 62
Lilacs / 66
Body, Earth, Water: A Meditation / 67

from *The Center for Cold Weather* (1989)
Living Next Door to the Center for Cold Weather / 73
In a White Absence / 77
Dancer among the Constellations / 79
Flowers / 84
To the Unborn / 86
A Seasonal Record / 88
Cleopatra Theodos / 93

August Arrival / 95

The Faithful / 97

from *Guardian* (1995)

Blues: Late August / 103

Poem for Marriage / 104

Who Knows / 106

The Story / 108

Seven Months / 110

Not Writing / 112

The Great Quiet / 113

Mother's Day, 1993: Hearing We Will Bomb Bosnia / 115

Raptor / 117

The Perfect Service / 118

Earth / 119

from *What to Tip the Boatman?* (2001)

The Owl / 123

Old Trick / 125

Solstice / 127

Noon / 129

That Year / 131

For Months / 133

White Primer / 134

Cutlery / 135

"as if mad is a direction, like west..." / 137

The Ruin / 138

Intermediary / 140

Reconciled / 142

After Persephone / 143

What to Tip the Boatman? / 144

The Return / 146

Persephone, Answering / 147

Demeter the Pilgrim / 148

Figure of Formal Loss: Pearl / 150

Fist / 152

from *White Sea* (2005)

Salt / 157

The Old Question / 159

The Source / 160

The Waiting / 162

Catalpa / 164

Cane / 166

Burial / 168

Want / 170

Moonsnail / 172

Death of a Gull / 174

Speech to the Self / 176

The Release / 178

White Morning / 182

You Must Cross the Black River / 183

Praise Him / 184

Soul / 186

from *Book of Dog* (2012)

Canis / 189

Ants Want My Yellow Moth / 191

Song of If-Only / 192

Their Chamber / 193

Essential Tremor / 194

In Lent / 195

Interstice / 196

Noise / 198

Book of Dog / 199

Salt Water Ducks / 209

Dune Shack / 210

Alone / 211

Western Conifer Seed Bug / 212

Survival: A Guide / 213

Acknowledgments / 215

Notes / 216

New Poems

THIS TIME, THE HAWK

Not safely away, that high-up glide
admired in day sky, and not even the off-guard
thrill of seeing the wild turkey's chick snatched
from the row in one easy swoop—this time,
straight and sure in the evening gloom,
it came at me. The hawk, diving
as I've seen in photos, headlong,
close-up: that curved beak, blunt-headed, wide.
I cowered, it swerved
upward to a broken-off trunk
not ten feet up. There, regarded me.

A real hawk, I thought. Nothing imagined
for once in these woods.
I could see dozens of burls in that trunk,
knotted boles where years of insects had burrowed,
the bark curdling and bulging. I didn't know then
how deep it lay in me, the illness
calling out, waiting for me in night's domain.

THE DIFFERENCE

Terrifying to have one's self give way—
old boat which has carried me around,
stubborn at the helm. Self the great
spirit-finder, haphazard navigator; in the end
a hand dragging in the water.
Energy, I thought, was her great strength, her voice
chattering under the whip of wind.
Meanwhile, out here in the complicity
and amplitude, brazen in their plainness,
fin and wing and wave
are one moment of action. Hawk takes off
with a nestling, then the hammering
dive of the plover's chase. Gull after gull
drops the clam on the rocky flats and knows how
to peck out the salty meat. Over and over,
nature does one thing, and this is the difference.
I who have lived my life intent on direction,
now I am blank. No destination after all.
And she whom I called *desire*,
called *must* and *act*—oh goodbye, that idea
striking me with her impertinence, her stone.

BED-BOUND

I live in the seam of stitches and throb.
Morning drags me back, insistent
ceiling fan above, dull blade
covered with detritus, spinning
to a vague thunder. Another day
ruled by water in the swell of air.

Time creeps. Eyelash, hangnail,
tapestry of moths laced to the screen.
The storm of tiny bugs
the heat brought in, hovering
over the skin of pockmarked fruit.
Meanwhile, the pill exacts its buzzing limits

and I lie here
with nothing but pain to consider.
A lens, intent on geography,
a personal weather
waiting out the day. And it is patient—
so patient, pain is.

AFTER CHEMO

They never expected me back.
Mice took the house,
burrowing into linens and tissues.
Vent or crack, they nestled in—

half an inch will do it. A bed
in the stove's insulation, clever
lacuna between the oven and fire.

I am not the same, and they know it.
Afraid of what I might touch
wherever I reach, connections
severed, all the lines chewed.

My house is a sieve. In and out they go
with sunflower hulls, cartilage bits,
nesting, nesting . . .
                    Winter will shut me
in with the stink, trapped with a Havahart
I can't empty. It's a matter of waiting.

NOT MYSELF

For the first time, I could see a link
between me and all the other
impossibly dead, or the ones who had gripped the dead
in their arms. The soldiers screaming *buddy, stay with me*.
Newspapers brought it all home: ruined men, their women
eyeing them. And the ones left, as if my kin,
dragging their bodies around on little sleds, lucky
encounters with land mines, numb as mothers
no longer counting days. No longer

did I gaze into the abandoned orchard's
frozen remove. What could be new
in the wind's blank resolve
cracking the branches? Or to think winter's clench
could have anything to do with finality.
Want was an unsolved puzzle
I threw away from my being. *Without* became
my *within*. Let's say I was no longer bound
to the old self: she hadn't known she could be broken.

DYSKINESIA

The wind blew up and over, cold
moved in. And that insisting
note trained on the lip of a bottle
teasing me with something beautiful.
May wind comes blooming,
dark side of dove-call,
spring's warning under the promise
of light at five a.m. Something
beneath birdsong flew the air
through the flimsy north-facing windows

and found me. First, it was a simple
tapping, mysterious argument
of my foot against the ancient floor,
then my right side with its jerk,
its skinny flimflam dance, crazy arm
obeying whatever spirit had flown.
Time now for my body's answer, the body
inhabited—how could I not fall?

THROUGH THE COFFIN WINDOW

In this old house, they moved coffins
through the witch's window on the gable end,
six feet of diagonal glass over the stairwell,
stippled with bug shit and guts, dried horseflies,
clots of the long-ago insect dead.
Whole histories have unfolded here,
but I keep missing the sea, the seamless
covering over and polishing.
Dust is what I slipped on.

What I remember: not the moment of the fall
but my body flying forward, hands clutching.
The air released me, threw me
headfirst into the wall. Black motes,
tiny travelers, followed a little trail ants made
to sugary specks of piled eggs
living in the floor where I writhed.
Pain did all the talking.
I was God's coward, trying to crawl away.
Then rescue came with the needle.

I was imagining death's door, one way
to turn me down the steep nineteenth-century stairs.
Head first, strapped in with morphine, sinking in
that deep water, they could take me

through the coffin window.
No need to keep the witch out
when she was already in.

MOTHER PAIN

Once in the vast middle of pain—pain stopped,
and a certain clarity descended.
In the sudden effortlessness of being, I could
forget the body. I stayed perfectly still,
caught up in wanting it to last,
this unexpected innocence born of the body's permission.
Minutes passed before I had to move,
and pain came riding back, rising and twisting,
this time trying to throw me across the room.
She was the big wind coming through windows I couldn't close,
turning over the orchids I loved, splattering the dirt.
If she wanted, I'd be on the floor weeks later,
still falling, and she'd bring the walker in to stay,
to remind me she owned it all. I was just furniture
that needed dumping. I was a dropped clock
and time had turned to serve her, my every second
belonged to her. She said *just die.*
Submission is not such a terrible thing: she knew
how to play me out with her pills, her bribes.
I give up I said, and that was how she knew
she could release me for those minutes
and I could be my own country, in charge of my little self—
the thinking and planning that had once been the sum of me.
Later, I could see how this leniency was only to show
how easy it was for her to get me back.
Mother, I cried, and cursed my infant cries.

9

THE NEWS AT TWO A.M.

It can make you crazy
if you listen to your heartbeat long enough.
But when I get up in the night,

it's not me, not really,
instead the one who flails and freezes. Her body
now some clumsy other.

Walking in this dark
is all about the wall. Try not to stumble
into the painting of the sea you love; don't hit

the dune shack photo you've sent flying.
Keep your roving hands

waist-high if you can. Go slow, I tell her,

travel the wall, the comforting law of the wall
keeping her upright, straight, shuffling
my steps like a drunk, feeling my way

for what little thing might trip her—
trying to make it down the hall
with nothing more than bruises.

All this trouble with pronouns
comes with having been taken over: *you*, *me*, and *her*
divided by news I can't fathom.

ARM, ETC.

Arm has become her own machine
stuck on the job of reaching, all the rules broken
in some other language dragged from the depths.
The brain's got secrets that even
arm doesn't know. Arm no longer cares for

anything hand might want to do, and hand
gets pulled along. Sullen child, poor hand
caught in a vise, stiffened by its throb and drum.
Arm still insisting, holding hand behind my back,
mad tap-tapping to keep from being dragged away.

What a story: me walking with a stick
along the beloved beach, and arm refuses, starts up
directing the waves, flying out in the good
beach air, as we all try to look away. Can't stop,
says hand. Can't balance, leg says. This is how
the body wakes me up and this is how she knocks me down.

This sorrow is all about my mother:
Did I not believe her stuttered
spoon-to-mouth, soup on the floor? Her level black eye
entering me. She could slap my face now,
hand could, in this boring chorus of saying.

But sometimes hand flies up to pat my shoulder
or curls close by my side, pretends to sleep—sweet pet
doesn't want arm to make me weep.
Then when I start to forget, hand
runs off, slams the glass, the plate, the sink.
And as for the little slave fingers—in the grab, they just let go.

WHAT THE KNIFE IS FOR

I think sometimes of that desperate child,
and wonder if now I'm paying
for her lies. So easily punished
these days, I've learned to pay attention
to what's real, and the knife is

a lesson to remind me. The sting
on my unsuspecting hand,
ambiguous in its direction as it releases
the knife or slides its blade into my palm.
Even before I can slice it, the bubbling pie
slips out of my grip, broken glass flying.

Again tonight, drowsy in thought,
and hungering for an apple's keen edge,
hand and knife conspired. They bring me back,
they want the little cry
that comes before the blood.
A gleam and a slip of a cut
parts a knuckle, opens a vein.

MOTHER

When I can't walk I think of you. I catch
your light in my mirror and see it
find my sallow cheek, the failing line
of jaw. Without looking, I can feel
that grimace or wince overtake me,
just a second's worth of you
in the future of my face.
Nothing fails to remind me—a finger on my arm,
a twisting in my back when I turn too fast
and fall. Tired of my arrogance, you are behind me
with time to show how you felt
to be a shell left empty and waiting.
So it is that I steer my body out of the crowded
what-has-been. Because of you,
I've come to love a broken thing.

SPRING

I can see the reasons for leaving,
how the stutter of foliage, archipelagoes
strung through what's left of winter's meanness,
is not enough. Hopkins said God's grandeur
would hold us, but his room is too bright
for all the bodies of the dead. Add them to the smaller
tragedies exploding in our hearts,
the needle in the remark, the faltering
on this side of a lie, or worse,
the boy or girl your own child loved.

On this day when spring is waiting to happen,
big questions matter—joy here, misery there.
But I am mired in my ignorance, insistent
on my small studies of selfhood. So closely I regarded
what is dependably lovely—that living tinge
under the icy scrabble, then rain overnight
and one day's sun brings the snowdrops up.
Best to turn away from those green stems
as they push through.

UNFINISHED

No death like the death you do not see; that moment
inhabiting the stilled body. Better to have a body to bury,
the young man who comes back
hammered shut in a box, the stony-eyed family
telling his last stories. Parts of stories, carried forward,

the way we repeat my brother's last goodbye,
walking out the door on a warm November night,
mother in the kitchen. *I'll just be gone awhile* . . .
And so the nightmare of the missing begins, so the mind
needs to invent an answer. Years we keep
going back, looking until absence
has become my brother's name, and in his place
a certain repetition: swamp and quicksand,
a sinkhole for easy dumping, ugly words
that won't sing like *bayou*. "Blue Bayou"—
my brother when I last saw him
on the back porch, picking out the tune. The mind keeps
trying to fool itself, as if there is no real death

but the one we can see coming, the one that gathers
the family together, the peace
offered by the very old, who lies there, accepting,
while we wait and hold the hand, then let it go.
But I was not there to see my mother in her bed
asking only for my brother

as the others stood around her, the ones who said
what they needed to say. Blessed ones,
you who knew what there was to say
and said it.

THE YEAR

The time will come—meanwhile you'll add more ashes,

that dirt in your hand. Goodbye, goodbye,

you'll learn to say it. What you want is

dirt on the coffin, ashes in the grave.

Not a glimpse, year after year, of someone on the street,

turning a corner before I can see

that red plaid shirt, torn sleeve. Tender twenty-six,

bad number, risky year of secrets.

Half that and it's thirteen: my boy at the memorial

playing Chopin, over and over, the waltzes, the preludes. My son

who kept on playing in the dim chapel, the child he was

repeating for want of what to do next,

waiting for permission, all his elders like stick figures

stuck there, stunned and seated,

until I rose, whispered in his ear. As I am whispering still,

his age now the same as the brother he played for: my brother

with no body to bury. And now

I've made a service for our mother,

sealed in her carved box, the censer's smoke

of ashes, the chanting Greek, no classical repertoire

from my son, twenty-six, as I keep saying,

dear God, let him double his life and double it again.

THE RIVER

This is the way it starts: her son
stretched out under a white sheet on the morgue's steel table.
For one second, two thoughts: *not him*:
he sleeps on his side, and then,
what can that sheet be hiding? Closer, she sees
it is her son, same son in his same skin,
unbroken, unmarred. *Un Un Undo this.*
But what becomes undone, she thinks, is that which is
still becoming, because to live is always
an act of becoming, an act of change.
He passed, she says, the words a dam
holding it back. Now months have given way.
Without storm, no visible unmooring,
she finds that she is on a river, caught and carried.
Some days sweeping her under,
she wakes to fight the current; a dizziness
sends her flying across the surface,
slams her flat. Other times, the roiling
well beneath, she floats in a kind of calm,
buoyed by the grace of strangers who knew him,
and goes about the details of keeping
her son's life as if he still lived it.
The river moves on, insistent on its course
through the highs and lows of the delta,
taking all the little tributaries with it, the bayous,
every waterway opening and closing—

unceasing, breathing secret of the river.
And she has come back from there, radiant companion
to everything she will never know—*I was lucky:*
I saw my son and he was beautiful.

GOING UNDER

One more step toward the wave, as though
I need evidence of this world going under.
Everything tells me how much worse it can be,
having come to the point that murder, like everything else,
has a rank and file. One thing about horror:
the more you know it, the more
you can't bear. No one wants to hear
the actual gun firing, the camera
catching it all, as it did in North Carolina
this morning. My daughter teaches
her class of five-year-olds: *we practice emergency*
because a big mean animal might get in the building
and we have to hide. How much easier,
in this fall-filled Vermont weather, to have a slice of pie,
and when winter does arrive, blizzard on the doorstep,
the driveway iced and pitiless, we could be in a bowl,
protected by the sum of things, locked in.
Watching the small worry of a bird
struggling to fly through the white onslaught—
oh so much easier, even a flock of frozen birds.
And how to put that next to
a child's version of the world going under,
good, bad, and the lesson of love. That one
small word, light enough to carry around.

BROKE

A rescue horse you'd train
first with the strap across her back,
lying there with the weight of something benign,
then days of resting an arm there
before you lean your whole self in. The mare,
without a mean bone in her body,
all goodness in a gray so white you want to believe
the sun has settled in her withers.
And after the weight of birthing
a lovely filly in a summer of good mothering,
after years of who-knows-what has kept her alive,
she eyes you with something like trust.
But all fall, growing gaunt, she has stood
in the weather, head down against pain,
her manure turning liquid and rank.
No complaint, as if the rain has become another
sensate being, the fog a companion,
and she an extension of the meadow
fed to a green splendor. Despite the verdict inside,
her coat has thickened, shiny
where her ribs show through, skin strict
over the jutting plates of her hips.
So quiet, she stands, as if to say she's ready now
for the saddle, reins, the pressure
of a gentle knee, the slightest tug
that will turn her in the direction she needs to go.
And you will take her.

THE OLD SELF

I have always loved the world, wanted the world
to love me back, though I see this was a bargain
I tried to make, some effort toward God
I thought was necessary. All my life it has been
one exchanged for the other   if this, then that.
Once running at dawn I stood on a precipice
overlooking the summer Atlantic, thrilled to tears.
Tears made it real, that earnest pulsing beauty below me
making me a part of the alive and purposeful.

Now when I wake to pain, there's no path
but the one leading to submission.
Pain has claimed the territory, bringing down
the flags—love, ambition, promise—
the formerly beautiful country made of belief.

THE BODY, FULL OF BIAS

Having, as I do, some preparation—
my dead toes already
testing the edge of another world—

when the loved one keeps me
tight in his arms, believing
he is strong enough, I want to turn away,

unable to bear his loss of me.
My body has traveled somewhere
indifferent to his care, though I try

to call it back to what I know is home.
If it's revenge my body wants, I do
confess a conceit I've nourished, always

striving to be better, the best, the *me* of me
always in motion, disregarding whatever
the body might need, its shade obediently following.

Now when I try to cross the threshold,
my feet stutter at the doorframe,
though I push and press; my protesting

arms fly forward, and stuck there I can't
coax my legs to follow. No matter
that the loved one waits,

urging on the other side.

Big step, he says with all his dear effort.

And the body looks on with pity and regret.

BEING APART

Again, some new curiosity turns me
this way and that. If I leave for a few minutes,
the world changes, resisting my hold on time;
it is a planet after all, with its own moon
and the night's business to do. I catch myself
wondering how to say goodbye.

But I am tired of goodbyes, as I am tired of trying
to resist. The infinite variety of the same
wakes me every day, this illness that makes me see
myself apart from all the rest.
Around me, there is always more—at this moment
jackhammers clatter away in the street
as a hulking machine lays down new pavement
over cracks and holes.
So much work to keep us from falling.

And it's comforting to go into the water at its peak.
I've seen the bottom—I know it's there,
as I know the submerged rocks, the exact
location of the boulders' decided row.
I could be shoved against them—thrown.
Tonight under the tropical sky, colors of a bruise,
the indifferent on-going tide
shuffles in, one hour at a time.

AFTER THE BODY

What end of waiting, what possibility,
when I believe in some transforming spirit.
I look to the obvious butterflies, the iridescent
glob of eggs the frog left in the brief pool,
even the webbing of spider mites and the red
pirate bugs that eat them. I assign too much hope
to the smallest breakable creatures,
crying over the bird that dashed itself into the glass
and lies there wasting in old snow.
I am in that bird, that dirty clump on the road.
And the larval skin of the emerging dragonfly,
all eyes and clutching, split
from its own cells and newly winged.
How can I protect it, the time it will need
hanging there, waiting for its wings to dry?
I have been a mask, a ghost, breaking out of myself
into all those bodies.

SILVER

The design, I see, is extraordinary.
Why watch for hummingbirds when I am caught
by the spider web strung in three layers
outside my kitchen door. Silver linking silver
fence, its chain anchoring one end, the roof's
overhang studded twice. A geometric pattern,
a trick of the light this hot morning
after a hot night. The net holds
a constellation of tiny bugs, inconsequential
flights that ended here, a white moth
spinning, and as I look closer,
three long silver hairs—my own
I have to assume, migrated from my deck chair
and made pure and purposeful.

I'm in a kind of sleep, so think to free
the fluttering caught thing.
The moth's wing falls off in my hand.
Poor thing, I tell myself, *wake up.*

Selected Poems

FROM

Aerial View of Louisiana

(1979)

AERIAL VIEW OF LOUISIANA

The delta lies unchanged, flat
as childhood: a woman gathering pecans
from a yard black with water, purple martins
after mosquitoes, all winter mock lilac.

In the dream of wrought iron
you find them—the grandmother is fierce,
both arms waving you away. Your mother
takes your hand to speak
of fishing from low pine flats,
how she loves the nests of water.
She says your pride will be her death.
You wear your grandmother's wild name,
her fan of hair.

You wake to mountains: reflections
off coastal islands, hills of prairie marsh.
Memory is the first claim,
you'll spend your life coming back
to this flatness. By dusk you have forgotten
everything but the bleeding outline
of the river. You watch for New Orleans,
the white cluster of tombs.

FOR MARIA

The hot nights I slept with you,
a leg thrown across your back—
you never complained.
When our stepfather raved, I fought.
You didn't cry with me,
preferring the dog and marshy field.
I thought you lived in your own world.
Now what I know best about you
comes from that night at supper in the hot kitchen.
You clenched your teeth as long as you could
against his slash of belt
on my bare foot. But when the blood came,
you screamed in my place, *Bastard, bastard!*
and stopped us all.

Later in bed, we heard the words of our stepfather
through the wall, the breaking of our mother
who couldn't come to us if we called.
Next to the window, you faced the ledge;
the honeysuckle told lies
as you put out your hand, all night
held the small flowers.

AS YOU STALK THE SLEEP OF
MY FORGETTING

Again, I walk into the cluster of bayou trees,
the gray bark stripped by deer.
This far south, winter repeats itself
in rain, keeps the land half marsh.
You are hunting, quail at your belt,
covered by the chatter of birds
and small game. Again I try to guess
your exact place in the pine
and cypress, avoid your steps,
the aim of your gun.

Later you'll hide yourself
in those I trust: this man, that woman.
Always I am called back to you.
By now I have lifted heavily
my body's dark sleep, and I know
it is not that other house.
You are not doing your Indian walk
into my room, where I hold my body
tight against my breasts,
body wrapped in wool.

You can no longer touch me.
Still I stalk that land
where I will find the safe bodies you have taken.

And I must finally hold the knife
against their throats, must uncover you
in those ragged trees, and fight myself awake
into this northern cold,
the house secure in snow
that is still falling.

A PLACE OF ANOTHER NAME

I speak from this location, the present
where I wake with a rosary of names
in a place without fig or mimosa.
A forest is collecting here,
straight as bone that forms the dead
even when the dead are gone. Around me
the hours fall into themselves.
I wear another history, a box of flesh
is how I keep it.

I am surrounded by those who know
their descent, who bring back generations
of names. My veins are muddy,
willed by my grandmother
with an olive tree from Mytilene. She gave me
the name never given, won't let me forget
my obligation. I carry her in my clothes;
she wraps me, a garment sewn with stones.

But she is bones away in another skin,
a place of another name. I drag myself
into the frame of the present.
My heart winds itself daily, I need the calm
of lead. I consider the rock passage
to a water where birds fly low
and lighter, lifting their wings.

I say this into the mouth of the future
with its vacant measure of time, past memory
that holds us to names. From marrow of edgebone
to white moon of nail, I am tenuous,
claimed by the touch of faces,
hands loose as rain. In this life
I learn to stay north, I search
a way to go. All the days end as water.

BEES

Mad with venom, they fly between the layers,
revealing the crevices in the brick.
I wake to the fine instrument of their hum
prisoned in the heart of the house.
Why did I disturb the nest they wove from themselves,
spray poison in the spaces over the door?
They dragged their egg sack into the darkness of the wall.
Even the crippled hatched; hundreds
crept out, struggled to fly.

They beat on the windows and fall on the burning stove.
Open screen, open door—nothing takes the smell.
Every morning I stomp the buzzing
along the floor. My bare feet find their litter,
find the dead ones with their tiny stings.

I tried to live with the bees
as I have in my flawed house, tried to ignore
the ragged black mole in the center of my back.
But they have come to stay, half sisters
nagging at my body, and that singing:
they break my silence to die.

The bees hammer at my house.
They swarm in the walls, searching a new cavity,
as if to make a honeycomb, full and rich and deadly.

39

GETTING OUT

That year we hardly slept, waking like inmates
who beat the walls. Every night
another refusal, the silent work
of tightening the heart.
Exhausted, we gave up; escaped
to the apartment pool, swimming those laps
until the first light relieved us.

Days were different: FM and full-blast
blues, hours of guitar "you gonna miss me
when I'm gone." Think how you tried
to pack up and go, for weeks stumbling
over piles of clothing, the unstrung tennis rackets.
Finally locked into blame, we paced
that short hall, heaving words like furniture.

I have the last unshredded pictures
of our matching eyes and hair.
We've kept to separate sides of the map,
still I'm startled by men who look like you.
And in the yearly letter, you're sure to say
you're happy now. Yet I think of the lawyer's bewilderment
when we cried, the last day. Taking hands
we walked apart, until our arms stretched
between us. We held on tight, and let go.

PADRE ISLAND

You could be lonely here
forever, that sanctuary of cries
something to live for, the smell of dying
sea life almost loving.
Nothing that lives wild
asks for mercy, the silent fish,
the sacrifice of birds.
                    You'd never stop seeing
through that water. Consider the branches
and limbs around your face, the obscuring
moon, how you fight each loss.
You'd clear yourself
here, limited to the flat
open white, egret and pelican
taking their innocent food. Nothing's permanent
but this, the unbroken
cartilage of fish reappearing.

Compare your inadequate spine,
its frail anger, the empty arch
of your foot seeking strength. The skin,
a delicate memory whose recital of cold
you never forget. Think how you've been changed,
debts your body can't overcome, the humor
of your devotion. Here, the ocean owns itself,

wild geese mate for life. And you, trying

to make yourself necessary,

while around you the birds answer their true and final lives.

FROM

The Bottom Land

(1983)

BLACK WALNUT

Tonight I arrange on my table six apricot halves
with a nugget of walnut on each open center.
Then place, alongside, dates whose hollows I fill
with whole almonds. I begin to eat them
without ceremony, having considered each apricot
given its gold, its tenderness.
The glossy black dates need nothing, yet I want
them to cover the defiant husks of the almonds
hiding their milky flesh, which some people bare
by blanching in boiling water. The body
of the almond will split straight through
if left carelessly in the heat.
As for the walnuts, I don't have the usual
cultivated variety, meatless and blond
and meant to be beautiful, but the country-grown
black walnuts that feed on the packed red dirt of the South.
When people there feel a certain heartsickness
they go out in secret and eat that clay
to cure the hunger of grief. This is why
the tree grows with a quiver in the wood,
tightly grained under the meager canopy of leaves.
And the fist of each nut, revealed in its pulp,
will open only to a hammer's beat. The tooth
must spare nothing as it bears down,
righteously taking whatever it needs
to leave the hunger behind.

FOR BLUE

I don't forget.
I recognize the bruised persimmon of your lips
on others around me. And if I never
see again the sweaty ribs when the body bends,
there's you, picking from can't-see to can't-see.
And your fingers on the nape of my neck
when I'm about to wake. So when I call
my own girl *Blue*, it's after you,
it's for your one pale eye, shadowed
and blind as far back as I go. Lucille,
black French of your voodoo mother with airs,
that high yellow you cursed is almost my color
in your skinny lap—your hand on my belly
to feel the flicker of the tiny tail
of another girl you said would grow there.
Black butterfly, the shoulder's twitching bone,
you crouch in the roadside ditch
for morning clay, that last remedy
to satisfy the ambiguous craving of the poor.
What you called a misery in the heart
wakes you. I almost always have a fever
and you put the fire in the glass
and the glass on my back. You are humming
to that purge and the circle eats the flame.
I am tasting your milk again, Annie Blue.
I'm tasting your spit and your black neck

like a clove in my mouth. And the good days
of sweet tea, hot water bread
gold in the pan, the carp and their liquid eyes.
The body is another kind of earth.
I don't forget what you fed me.

BODY, EARTH, WATER

There's a tree and what I know
is that some part of it is always dying.
In every storm another wing of cypress
goes down. Though I tie my branch with knots
of evil eye, I can count on a symmetry
ruined by August, sure as the Purple Hulls
we plant and the saturated cane
on the colored side of the parish.
The rain makes windows in the ground
and I know by now he'll step anywhere.
I'm a girl with big long legs, ashamed
of the way my brother lays himself out,
partly submerged on the wavering
roots of the cedar. I still have a thin white line
tracing my right heel, split by the callus
that rose up like a boat for the foot. Devil's work,
says the woman who warned against water's touch
on my new female self. I fear for days
my slip off the branch lacing the creek—
that separation not so crucial,
as years later seeing mountains I expected more
height and a certain resolution.

Landing in the cotton field in Ouachita
I see those windows flash their futile vacancies.
Once I saw my brother

take off his clothes to a whole afternoon's mutiny of light and rain.
God help me from making a universe here:
this will I give the water
to fuse together and split apart, the punishing
quadrant of the hurricane that never raged
north of Baton Rouge.
I'm looking for a form,
a face that won't dissolve. Where's the boy,
the woman, the red clay I learned to squeeze
through my fist to clean it?
She put that dirt in her mouth,
a hunger and anger nothing will take out of me.
Some current still brings down
the stand of cypress. Show me earth,
that's what I say to my brother, though I know
I give those trees their order, and nameless, too,
the fringe of vine and bird, the improvident cage
woven around him.

ELEGY FOR THE OTHER

For Jimmy, killed November 1979.

I.
Four a.m. and still snowing,
far from the bottom land
where the creeks eddy and deepen to swamp.
Someone is crying down there and I call
come back, but the body does not rise
or wave those arms which are limp and torn
in the mud. I cannot see the face
receding into black, only one
devastating mark, the stained forehead.

You are not here, not in the mottled light
of February. And this icy pond
only reminds me of another, swollen by now
in the muddy rains. Across the lilac cold
I see you in the trees' black
against white, see you shrug and turn.
And if I run, clumsy in the crusted snow,
ragged breath rising, it will be to find
some child's sled upturned, a jacket swaying.

I wake and sleep in one long breath,
breath of rain that falls and falls.
You are a child again, my reflection,

carrying a pail of berries,

black raspberries that never grow in the heat.

Smiling, you show me where they are hidden

on land no longer familiar to me. And the voice:

take them, we are alive. But when we enter

the knotted pine kitchen, I find the berries

furred in the bottom of the pail, impossible to save,

and cry out in my way: *ruined,*

see what you have ruined,

and in your smile see everything I have refused.

North and South again—through those months

the earth turns back and denies, I am still sister

calling brother. Come back, I say

as if to some change, not the bitter quiet of supper,

not the last wing of light

failing the path I search, vine and bramble

threading the marsh that circles the town.

2.

I expected more than a reed broken

in the rain. I thought you would rise up

with your fists, the pistol

radiant in your belt, badge of that country,

all the boys in their flannel shirts.

I would have dragged you out of there.

You, so good at turning your back,

knew full well what happens. Even when you'd quit

the dealing, the bar fights, the jails—

you called it *legacy.* The curse

is what we'll never know for sure, not without a body

to give us back its story—how they took you
out to some pecan grove or the endless pines
in November's first chill. This time

they emptied more than buckshot in you.
Them, with their deer rifles, wads of tobacco
and the spitting, every grudge
a smirk across the face. And the bastard
who tapped his gun on my wrist: *you won't ever*
find him, then waved over the line of trees that marks
the northern boundary of the endless bottoms.

When I can pray, this is my prayer:
that you went out with one pure breath,
the stroke of an arm reaching, as in flight
that unexpected beat when the long white
feathers of the nightjar open.
                              This prayer
against hatred, this prayer for grace:
that you were blind and deaf
so could not give them back themselves;
that with their touch, the intricate
cage of your body collapsed. Irrelevant,
the passing of flesh into those hands.

Night after night, I lie down cold
in that life again, where nothing has changed
in the opaque stillness, the dry sound of insects,
smell of swamp musk and lime.
If I could only let the darkness cover you,
a kind of coat but penetrable,

the way water is a garment
opening its arms to hold you
and hold you, until your face is the swamp's face
and there is nothing left to understand.

3.
The difference in our life
was how it stripped childhood bare.
How to endure the knock-upside-the-head,
hands tied under the table, the particular
taste of fist against teeth,
blanks fired behind you, blood against metal.
God knows I fought for any reason
except you, born the same
dead center of August, 1953:
your birth, our father's leaving.

Not so high above me, but unreachable
in the mimosa, that blossoming house.
And our sister with you, your secret
language I saw as denial. You hid
and were found: stepfather, the neighbor boy
with his ropes. Forgive my indifference,
forgive me my fear, which was how I lived.
If something in you closed
and never healed, I know what I didn't give,
not the cracked papershells in the pecan tree,
the rare hawthorn's mayhaw berry...
Maria remembers the afternoon the three of us
played in the house alone. She found a box in a drawer,
like some kind of gold and filled

with things. Held up to the sun
they were trinkets. But how we made them ours,
laughing; the give and take of light.

Forget it, you said: months of limping
and the Saturday morning I found you
stiff-legged, white. The year on your back,
hole in the heart, you learned those things
we never thought to name in Tremont Bottoms—
lifespans of the water turtle, the white-tailed
deer who live out their flawed lives
prey to the hunters' misfire and every bodily affliction.
The last time I saw you, we drove out to the hill country
around D'Arbonne Swamp and its expensive
false lake. I took some deep velvet buds
from a friend's pasture and put them in your truck,
thinking I'd find some rare name.
Sumac, you said, brother to poison, but this one
called staghorn, for the bare antlers the branches make
rising out of winter.

4.
I am frightened of this sleep, the way it holds
and pulls under the child I carry,
the one I will abandon to save myself.
You walk, unreachable above water,
and this time I am the one calling from below
until nothing will catch me
and the child too falls away,
growing smaller every time I dream.
My arms ache and release. *I can't carry us both*

I scream and you sink. Your eyes wide
and calm, you sink.

I powder the ugly leaves of mullein
and throw them on the water. The stunned fish rise,
your body rises. I collect the broken pieces
so the soul can reach
the forgetful region of sky.
All night I sift and pick, I separate
our skinny fingers, handfuls of our hair.
I count, I fit you together in a box.
What is flesh but silt? And what is nail?
Here's the softest bone,
box of water, box of air.

Give me back the face in the mirror,
the cup by my bed. I am not the eye of your mother,
the arm of your father. Don't come to me
wearing your face like an emptiness I must fill.
For the last time, I'll wrap you in my skin,
carry you home. I'll lay down
your bad heart, the ox-blood boots.
I'll bury my lack, my failure.

5.
We are staring with different eyes
into the maze of leaning cypress.
No longer children, we question
every detail, the tangle of snakes
jarring the surface,
the way our toes curl into the mucky ledge.

We are waiting to see
Audubon's snowy birds unfold
their ruffled feathers: pelican, egret, owl
lifting over the promise of water.
I can hear the sound of a clacking,
dry branch in the cedar, the snow
stripped away by wind; a louder
and louder creaking, as though every door
to this house has been broken. Then the wind
in the old tree subsides until it is
the sound of walking through the uncut field,
until it is night again
bringing another change in season.
If I stay up long enough, then you will come as well,
wearing the preoccupied mask of the dead,
that cast of light. I know you are dead
because your eyes reflect water,
because all water is the sound of crying.
Though I can't hold you, I lean into the white
wall of your body and you lull me,
somnambulant. You are the secret of sleep,
your face with its fine grasses and moss.

Out of the northern spring
with its unmistakable signs of rain, of birds,
I come back.
Back through that religion of night sweat
and heat, the religion called South,
called family. Back through dark—
thin slice of swamp moon, sumac
and sweetgum turning, creek water,

whisky in the clear glass.
And in them all I find you. You
the master of disappearing, the artist
escaping burial, the trick of guilt.
And if I become more graceful,
it is that I am a shelter for your absence,
the smoothness imposed on rock
worn away from within, the force of water
in its essential movement. This is how I keep you
and this is how you break away,
leaving tear, blood, seed.

WHITE FIELD

Denial, because the body
wants to trample what it cannot bear.
And how rage consumes that field
burning in dream light, where again
I sit with my brother
among the endless meadow-rue.
And it is he who is so kind
as I make my usual fist,
shaking and pointless, because I know
death has given him this smile
that has nothing to do with me.
I cry harder, dressed in the faded
working clothes he's cast away,
the muddy boots; his hands and eyes
my own, though we are no longer the same.
And I cannot hold him back,
not by arm, by word, the way I stomp
the everlasting whiteweed; the body
turning to gunshot,
the body falling.

ON THE TWELFTH OF MARCH

I am finally quiet, listening
to the clumps of snow release the house,
the silence given over to ducks clattering
in the freed pond where they crouched for weeks
on snow-covered ice. This new snow falls
without heart to hold to limb or stone.
The earth has had what it can take
and wants to rise out of its old shell.
If I could, I too would create some beginning.
I would walk out into the white curtain
that hangs like a border between grief and forgetting
and let the snow gather again, flake by flake
building its tiny monuments on the blades of grass,
on each brown-scarred flower of the dogwood
ready to open like the palm of a hand.
I would let all things of the past merge
as one, as every substance of a field is covered
without detail. And I would say: it is all here
beneath me, unchanged yet hidden.
I would walk until the cold
made me a part of the closed ground,
until the crow in my heart rose.
Maybe then I'd want these furled March buds
that stubbornly bring themselves forth, the broken
calendula already opening. I'd accept
what it is I've left here, the cicatrix
gleaming beneath the snow.

FORT WALL AT MYTILENE: GREECE, 1921

Hearing of their deaths, my grandmother returned
to stand on the wall of the fort, nameless
at Mytilene. It marks the hilltop, defender
as ancient as God's blessing or the eye
that casts off evil. In her black-feathered bag
the letter she had brought that far, which she ripped
and let go, particles lingering in the blue air.
She had come to gaze past the battery
guarding the Turkish bay, to Ayvali,
where the Greek colony had been cut down,
their blood final on land so close and foreign.
And when she cried out, hearing the short bell
that summoned those people to their noon prayer,
it was for her mother's scattered bones, each sister's
fine hair, a fabric woven from death on death.
Nothing has changed on that stark wall
where in the noon glare no outline of a woman or man
is ever hidden, and in the land's silence
no sound will cover the force of gunshot,
a body obliterated into the rocky hillside.

These are dangers I don't understand.
Though I know why she went back there
to walk up the circular road in her tight-laced shoes,
the black scarves, a young woman looking over water
she had so recently crossed. She spat on her finger,

rubbed it across the dusty lid of each eye,
she made the sign of the cross three times.
Mother, sisters, brother, the whole cloth of their bodies
ripped away. And because the men still gathered there,
some given up for lost in a war which never ceased,
she would stay to search for them
among the stunted trees, olive or dry pine,
learn to bury them in the broken road
where her ancestors had laid the rough white stones,
plutonic rock taking its red cast from the years—
the granite she'd carry.

MOON AND STARS OVER CRETE:
FOR ALEXANDRA

1.

Here are the stones saved in their water
from Crete. Here are the stars that swam in milk
over the balcony of geraniums, over the hotel,
the shabby town ten miles through dust,
the winding donkey path.

Behind fire thorn, the stark silence
of the land's climbing rock, lay the balanced
curving sea. I stood in the waves
and let the rocks rise and fall over my feet;
motion by motion they sank in the sand.
I wanted my flat body to take on an aspect of the sea,
as the moon recreates the sky and pulls us back
nightly, renewed in that wrapped veil of light.

2.

Perhaps the sky was so close the stars let go—
falling through the mirrored water.
Unearthly rocks, they lined the Mediterranean,
worn smooth, joined to the moving floor of the sea.
I wanted them, too far down to gather,
just as they had lain in the open current of sky.

Or I'd swim all the way down
through the layered shade for the perfect stone
and find its color had become part of that earth
which is the jeweled bottom of the sea.
I didn't know how deep you lay,
minute starfish in the sea of my body.

3.
So simple, beyond even dream, you
were floating above light
or rain or sleep, in a wreath of salt crystals.
The constellation repeated and repeated
while you changed each mask, separating
within my layered veils.

And before I knew: the first lens of the eye,
the brain shimmered in its bath,
intricate lace beneath the thinnest skin.
And the fine shells of the skull
rose up one by one, flower cup to hold the bud,
lonely fontanelle. You were a forehead,
you were a heart, you were a fish tail stirring.
Each finger budded from the web of your hand,
then the reaching shadow of the bone.
Then the calm of your face, waiting.

4.
In those first days, no thunder:
that faraway movement in the womb,
an absence of sound calling out.
Unchanged, the mountains hung over the town,

the valley of sea and rock. The sky brought forth
its metallic lights, each night
released the rain of stars.
Earth answered the moon's changing eye.

I wanted more than the smallest from the shallows,
the ones too lovely to reach.
I took what I could from that sea, stones
that gave away their colors to a milky film,
drank the water and dusted themselves green.
But I keep them for you, salt of the sky
inside me, sister of flesh;
how you learned to swim in your own tiny sea,
thrashing about your wrinkled feet,
finally pulled from the water of that tide.

5.
The moon reflects its silver atmosphere,
prize of a stone—
no bigger than the tip of my smallest finger.
Moon-nail, faultless curve, how you'll cry to have it,
to hold in your hand the perfectly lost.
Half-circle retrieved, the moon widens
to disappear, as the seas are taken away
and replaced; as you and I, one source
drawn apart, will be returned.

These are the stories I will tell you,
that we do not live in darkness
but an absence that can't be filled.
We sleep and wake, restoring a kind of sight.

The stars grow into themselves each night,
tiny and white above the beating sea.
When a star falls, unmerciful errand into water,
it blesses us in its flight.
And you, my daughter,
created in the water of sky and self,
will yearn for birth, again and again,
as we do in this life.

LILACS

They open before we have had a chance
to be unkind to each other.
In the dark the tiny whorls
unfold around the stem, candlelit
against the window; the infrequent dark
where our bodies gather and fill.
The lilacs bloom in their time,
the flowers dry in the billowing tree
which I will cut back
and further back.
                     What is desire
but a stone to bargain with? A longing
that says *be something else,*
until each holds the other
against change. The year turns,
the tree's frame empties,

empties again. If I could need
only what is given—
the way the limbs protect themselves
in spite of weather. Another dark
conceals the latent buds.
It's true, I am closed
between a past and future winter,
any fear made bearable when it repeats,
when it's mutable and brief.

BODY, EARTH, WATER: A MEDITATION

The land keeps giving up more land,
temporary earth. The straw-like kelp and copper weeds
catch upon the ridges, the bellied ground
exposed, marked with the prints of gull-foot,
the ceaseless debris of shell and black rust chain
something has to wash away.
I leap from patch to patch, the intruding
dead-colored land I use to get out here
into the dry sea, as if to enter
the same kind of heat that sweeps through us,

more than a tide shrugging off
the whisper of its monotone.
I'm hungry for color,
hungry for a water that won't turn away.
Say goodbye to me, that's what I'm here for.
Don't I know these flats, haven't I seen
current begging current, the river of winds?
I'm the one who got older. Nothing's changed

but these greening snake vines
and the fleshy pastels heaped like rags
swollen on the sea bed.
If I could love the land—
put my foot on the cold ground,
grateful for the smallest scratch,

some splinter I recognize
out here on the edge of the world.
These months I've walked back and forth
too early for sunrise, three blocks from house to sea,
saying *live here, this is where you live.*
Water, here's earth; body, here's blood.
If one's inert and fearful, the other keeps moving.
And over the full-bodied sweep of sea,
the long winter's moon—that mind
with its fickleness, its disclaimers.
Give me permission. Many-faced sister,
night's prize and medallion,
try not to care so much.

Nothing is going to save me from this body
and its careless assumptions. Some tic
will find me out, maybe I won't wake up,
a flood inside, the gut of me
submerged and drowned. The body
is no more than a wind-held bird
quicksilver over icy water, flapping
and flapping for the translucent gleam
of fish and the worm inside it.

Here's the shell I pulled out of a tide pool
and brought back to dry. One tiny membrane
swept out in the shallows of the sink:
a tail and an eye, vitreous pink. Newborn
pulse of the sea, spineless
wavering, blind push for the shell.

If we climbed out of some salty sea
then our sweat still betrays us,
this amalgam of body and water.
It's the metal taste in the scrape
on my thumb, the shudder of the broken
gull against sand, the half-eaten cod.
And when I slice the fish to see
the logic of its bones, eye matching eye,
it's duplicity I'm after. I make a deliberate cage.
Picking through the sea's rubbish,
I can see as though from some real shore
above the tidemark. The smallness of me
walking on land that will be sea in one hour.
And what I keep: the plum-centered spiral,
the in and in and in—to the roar, the sleep.

FROM

The Center for Cold Weather

(1989)

LIVING NEXT DOOR TO THE CENTER FOR
COLD WEATHER

It's more than you see: Cold Regions
Research Lab protected by its chain-link fence
on this street of prefab housing. And behind it,
the blank green knoll I can't get to,
a little field on the crest of the hill
and to the far right, an old cedar
like the one in my great-aunt's kitchen yard.
But the land behind the house
takes a steep dip into a kind of gouge
filled with waist-high scrub and razorweed
rising to a mangy tangle of poplar
that climbs the other side. There's no path
except the line some garbage-seeking skunk
or raccoon has pressed around the hill,

and all those over there are separated from me.
Young again, they speak—the aunts with their crochet
and warnings, my grandfather shaking his thin trees
hard to bring down the rain of olives.
And coughing Theo, whose knee is the first I remember,
the anonymous lifting me up.

                              It is the cough I think
that wakes me, the hacking in some faltering machine
that runs all night in the center for cold weather.
Windows and back door tight, it still invades,

sporadic over the whiter noise and hourly
thumping of some monitor for the gravity of cold.

Newcomer at the edge of an imposing winter,
what do I know about freezing, about thaws
of such shade and density they can take years.
I can't imagine a temperature as low as they claim,
weathering as I do these other reminders—
the family gestures, the particular
throw of the hand in the slaughter of lambs.
I see the small flaws in their skin, the mottled
red mole that finally killed one, another's birthmark
like one of Easter's red eggs.
Maybe I've brought them here to bury
under snow, up there in the serene heart of it,
away from the gray roadside clumps, the plow's
manufactured wall, or the news of pressure systems.

Maybe their presence is no more unlikely than
machines that measure cold and the fracture
thickness of ice. Some mornings I think I'll
put on the right shoes and take some kind of tool
to hack my way up there. Maybe then I'd see
beyond them, down the other side of the hill
to a river. Hills do fall away into rivers
and the Connecticut is nearby.
The water this time of year is low and still,
even warm, and I could lie down in it.
Looking back to this house
next to the industry of weather keeping,
perhaps I would see not so much the bleak yard, the fifties'

box housing in yellow, pink and blue,
but some shelter beyond the past.
I'd love this life for what it is,
intact, the simple day by day,
loved for its necessities;
no waking to the dread of what's lost.

Ask me what matters and I'll say
it is the nighttime of this place,
the time of weather change and cover, the hours
made of a small field and one tree,
the chilled room of sleep with the recurring
face of my thirty-year-old mother.

Nothing then has changed, yet outside
the drive of machinery
beats with the warp and turn of winter.
I am more a visitor on this street
than one who wakes at home in the center's
order of snow.
                    Sleeping to return, I find
the room where I made my first goodbye,
like communion or baptism, to provide
the ritual groundwork of my need.
She took me there to kiss him—
grandfather, his lips
dedicated to what passed between them:
breath and Greek, a tongue almost religious
in rural Louisiana. All night he sang the names
that meant a life to him. All night
the banded wrist rose and hesitated,

marking time with the hand
that would not be still.
Then sometime toward the end,
they pushed me to him. There resting on his chest
with the blue-veined wires, God's picture,
which I refused to kiss for the dying—
not yet knowing the season that assigns the heart its story.

IN A WHITE ABSENCE

Dull witness, I drag myself up—
out into a flat fog.
And like a fragment out of sleep's
incoherent bed, a blind man
comes tapping with a cane; emerging
out of the white stasis
to disappear. As he passes
I remember what part of this oblivion
woke me: running in a brightness
too false for sun or starlight, the dream-
yellow of a ruined photograph.
So when the pick-up slows beside me
I am not surprised to see him, my brother
in the blue-plaid flannel I wore all winter,
the thermal undershirt I dyed an awful pink.
I force myself faster, as if
to shrug him off, though he keeps
his face to the road and simply drives
beside me, increasing speed as I do.

What if he comes back,
not dead after all? Only a temporary
shying away from the necessary and lethal
family love. I am ashamed,
knowing how I would stammer, not with joy
for the lost returned, but the struggle

to justify my lies to the world. After years,
the old traitor, still spending my grief—
as if I could lose that, too.

White into white, where have I come to?
I reflect nothing, no distance, no light,
and there is no moon returning the earth's glow
in the face of so much goodbye,
not this morning.

DANCER AMONG THE CONSTELLATIONS

My shadow lasts two miles,
bitter in the gravel; our past confined
on this road where you found the monarch,
perfect and dead on the stalk of a weed
following the wind. A summer is nothing
in these mountains, a cloud is nothing, one more
jay's wing. So much for permanent weather,
the light I learn to do without—

as I learn *release* in this new season
tinging the other side of the ridge.
I run into the tunnel of trees, the last
degree of light; into the dead shade of the permanent
evergreen: black smell, black seepage
from the soggy ground. I'm running
for what the feet resist: my fault, my weight,
water and salt, anything
to keep from falling.

So what if it's beautiful—this sweet
color and smell of rot, of layers, night-wet
animal and bark. And when I plunge out of
the trees' black canopy, so what if the stars
blink above, redeemed and precise
in their tense formations. It's one more failure

not to love in my conspiracy of failures.
I'll make another marriage and give it
my whole self, like winter pulling in
the silver aspen and tamarack that alter
as I must alter the give and take of heart.
I'm running nights now, the black hours
for the killing cold; a shrug for need,
a shrug for what I gave, until I have no use
for the pain it takes to leave you.

~

Hands. They hang
white and dead, so cold
that absence outweighs sight.
I go on testing the *open* and *close*, a motion
that reminds me of claws
clumsy on the ocean floor;
my eye on the white muscle the fist makes,
the knuckles' blue ridge,
as if all evidence of the body
beat in the hands.
Pale blue: this light, this torch
in my side, and being
goes automatic, separating
foot from hill, higher and faster.
What I hear is the muffled slap
of running on snow, what I swallow
is bile and salt, my own gut self
rising like a ballast against
the cold body of the night outside.

Dead center: this heart,
this earth-planet
colored with thump; louder now
against the force field of my weight.
No brilliance here,
this systemic influence, this routine beat
eclipsing my tired feet in the snow.
Harmony goes dark and darker still
at the point of understanding—
what frost is to the cricket
or the postcoital stillness of the jay.
I'm home with this anarchy of hands,
this voice I can no longer shut up, something merciful
saying *leave it alone*: the seduction of grief
like a crucial cloth I've pulled away.
Now rain-runner, snow-eater,
I go face up in the halting mist, the stars
beginning to seed the long side of the sky.

~

You're meant to take the fall,
the penalty for thinking speed and grace.
Fool again, you give your weight
to what the foot can't hold, the dance
of loose gravel, and you go under
to motion's sheer waste. All you know
is slide and scrape. And it's like you,
this counting on pain
to say what matters: no love
is ever enough, and no safety

but in the lesson of failures.
You'll leave it all for the sake
of gut on bone. You'll burn
and all the luck you can ask for
is that someone close will hold you:
a handful from a small jar
emptied into the palm, cupped
as if for dust or oil.
From all its weight, your body
saved in a little grit,
then scattered into the wind: your pebbles,
the sharp and the smooth.

~

I run for change,
to learn the art of *now* and *wait*, to love
what's not a part of me—
fall's multitude of green, fall's rain,
I give up what the trees release:
sheer will and the time it takes
to understand regret, that whole music
in this haphazard season.

I run to leave the self
whose need I cannot bear,
for the tension in the body's beat and the dissonant
measure of quiet. For the lilac dome
descending and the rising constellations,
a solitude accepted
in the arc of shooting star. I chase

the brother in the body,
for the sake of wick and burning,
for the burning of the breath.
To stop the automatic counting,
free the song from its intent
and the being that contains the dance.
I free the foot thud
and the longing—freed
lightly for once,
as if it meant some careless rest.

This inconstant globe of light, the moon
blurred half among so many shapes:
unlikely swan, the arrow and the goat.
I exchange these candles
for every hesitation. And walk away—
exchange the passionate word
for sweat: this washing out of me,
seed and salt, anonymous
heat of any flesh,
and nobody's hand for comfort or intent.
I run for the closed
throat insisting, the clenching
in the waist, movement
as if there were no halt.
And for the far-off
figure of the runner,
flexed arm and fist, the rising
under these brief clothes—our bodies
mutual as they empty. Even from this distance
those leaps are my own.

FLOWERS

These blossoms outside the window
have nothing to do with the twentieth century.
Theirs is a foreign story,
more foreign than their name from the East,
since the East draws closer these days,
and their imposing health
belongs to a tree that thrives on its own.
What does the Chinese plum have to do with history,
the great public and private sorrows?
The present looms, assuming and yet
detached, the stems woven for the purposes
of their branches. The tree limits what I can see,
pulling me in to regard my ordered room,
so I cannot know the Vermont pastures
where the vapory rain of isotopes
bonds with compounds the grass drinks in
and the cows eat. My friend takes iodine,
on the safe side. What thick healthy flowers
distract me, what beauty bars the window
with its exclusive transformation,
not unlike government promises
on this morning of my grandmother's ninetieth birthday.
Seventy years ago, every member of her family
and an entire culture died at the hands of the Turks.
Flowers, she says, belong in the grave
where they cover the dead,

not the face of what we live.
My grandfather lived in this country
fifty years without learning the language,
yet never went back to Mytilene. He kept himself
surrounded by his gardens, his trees. His roses
meant nothing to her.

TO THE UNBORN

Quite simply, I gave you up.
I ran, and the miles lengthened
in my security of breath; my fear
less the neighbor's dog
than the buckling in my right knee.
Who knows when you began.
Summer gave itself to the beckoning fall;
apples ripened, though hail left them ruined
for market. Later the trees
shrugged them down. Windfall in the rich grass,
they drew a tinge of yellow and such flavor
we began to prefer the fallen,
barely noticing the tiny slug prints and brown
scabs of weather. Survival, after all,
is not an art, only an indication
of how little there is to trust.
I read this week how one child
spun into the Korean jet's ball of fire
somewhere over alien territory
and perished, a casual occupant
of the wrong plane. Still another,
just down the road, fell into one of the orchard hives
and died reacting to the common sting of bees.
In this way we all belong purely to the world.
Because nothing here means safety—
it's all territory we trespass,

and relentlessly. As that speck of you
lived on greed, the determined cells
multiplying to complete their plan.
It is enough to think of you
as I run in the still dark, your kin
cold above me. In that heaven
the stars move through their soliloquies
and the moon repeats. So much repetition
yet the shrug in any nature—as I your mother
would not give up my body to the long pull
of your survival, its futility and need.

A SEASONAL RECORD

I.
Spring, and so they danced
mid-air. He circled and repeated until she
paused to a second's locking.
Gazing by the window, dishtowel in hand,
I almost missed it:
red and gold, two velvets shivering,
then she was away. He perched
on the nearest branch; dead-still,
head cocked, as if to save the event,
while she went as usual among the trees,
chirpy and full of gesture.

Out the wrong door, he's on me
in a red flash, the cardinal with all his heart
wing-bent against me. He's driven
by what's required, something fierce in his gut
or in a shell. He needs to bring it out whole
and feed it, as he does his mate
waiting in the flowering plum.
He bangs the resistant feeder, flutters and grabs
the seeds meant for finches.

2.
Habit keeps me running around the empty nest,
my arc through summer and fall.

But this morning when I looked up
the viburnum's landmark of woven straw
was gone—leaves too, and color,
all the miscellaneous cover
that disguised the steep tilt of the land.
Now before the road goes pretty in snow,
I can see what I've been up against, that distance
to the bony orchard, and why it's taken
so much out of me to run it back,
suffering the green liar of the land.
As though it were some failure in me
that wrecked my knee or broke
the blisters on my heel. I look back
the way I've come: the mile climb to the barn
blacker than any summer cloud, rot-black, and see
no proof in my petty test of strength.

3.
Still driven by the astonishment
of destruction and renewal, I've gone down
panting in the orchard, a fool in snow
sinking in the hollows, and more snow
falling as I plod down the row of the counted
and diminished. At the end a few clear limbs
against the white population: one tree
with a wealth of apples not touched
in the ripe season. Having survived
the leaves, rain, and now blizzard,
they hang on, each day turning
a drier red, dark blood approaching
I suppose some final black, though no true black

exists in the plant kingdom.
The skin has withered around the juices, the flesh
shrunk to a little sap, yet they are whole—these apples
in their saving process of decay,
red enough to disquiet the empty land.

4.
Just another sparrow
and a January day. Give praise
to the dull, the predictable
good tiredness with which I sleep
the sleep of the dead.
Never mind the metal taste in my mouth,
my doubtful step on everything brittle.
This gray morning they all come back,
preening and diving at the feeder,
lured by suet or whatever I throw out
on the inch-thick ice. No thaw in this wind,
but something surfacing. And I am buoyed
by the equitable love of the living.

5.
A wet breeze, a melting.
My own face drips in this unearthing of snow,
the ground running with water
to release the cold. I come around
to the steep falling off of winter,
working harder at replenishing
the feeder. After three seasons
I can see what this nature's for: indifference
and a greed that doesn't go much further

than keeping the belly full.
It's a human need that keeps me
filling up the seed.
Mostly I've got nervous birds
and they're sloppy—but not these chickadees
bobbing at the feed in my outstretched palm.
In March it's the weather responsible
for the flat call of the grosbeaks, their fine yellow
in an evening cluster. One wing's grace
brings the last one down
to the dried sunflower I've tossed.
He tears out the seed and gulps it, the muscle
in his raised throat
swelling with perfunctory desire.

6.
On Mecox Bay, the swans
take flight out of running, an accidental music
made of wingbeating. They are fat as June,
their awkward breasts tipping forward,
waiting to play the single role of mother
hatching the greenish egg.
Opposing male and female, still they would join
for a hundred years. Why should they be true
as I long to be? And why does the afternoon
share sun and moon, both lights
equal on the opposite sides of a bay
too wide for me to run? I flail my arms
and whistle, trying for imitation.
The swans approach, sidelong, evasive.
I hold out one hand

for balance, webbed outline framed in light,
and with all my weight
throw the white pieces out, calling
come to me, swans, eat my bread.

CLEOPATRA THEODOS

We had language between us: her trick
of pretending not to know English
when she didn't want to speak. I pretended
not to know Greek, and so it went
that way for years, a clear standoff
in which she learned to get what she wanted
by staring deep into my face; the easy
track of my childhood never lied.
Her reward was my affliction: sties
flowered in my eyes. Around the iris
red flamed its way, evil she could see
settling in the rim. She knew some magic words,
province of one firstborn protecting another,
and she gave them, chanting and gesturing,
her face transfixed by mine.
Whatever the devil is, he listened
to her voice. She lured him out
into her atmosphere and pinned him to the meanest year:
to the twenty-four hours her first child lived
and the scimitar's blade in her mother's belly,
its few minutes of wrath against hidden children.
Five in a nation of murdered children
came back and spoke, safe for once
in the sanctuary of her face. Held there in Ayvali,
stone's throw from the ancient cities of grief,
the devil met his history. His gift for division

could not stand up to the power of her losses.
He would keep coming back with his attempts
to burrow in, to follow the light
through the optic nerve leading to the back of the brain,
to that tiny center where the soul is housed.
But no matter how he tried
to fix the fine point of his greed,
she lifted my chin and studied the possibilities:
the little tear ducts beginning to swell,
some threat of cloud in the innocent blue.
Over me, she spoke for heaven. Words opened
her hands and bound me to her.
With that music, with the light of her eyes,
she whipped him, dismissed him, and he fled.

AUGUST ARRIVAL

I am too happy for poetry,
too happy to abandon
midsummer, my children and flowers, so much
milk and fruit against the dreamy
backdrop of the northern mountains.
Like the first red twinge in the maples,
the usual acts of contrition
threaten to pull me out of this world,
but I am just this once at the center of it.
Caught in the precise moment of August,

something brings my brother back
to the instant of birth and the light's
old miracle. I think how Jesus must have
spoken to Lazarus: *rise now,*
rise; the sisters touching his robe as he passed,
ecstatic to see him truly alive and whole, as if
all his life had followed a straight line
to the affirmation of that moment. So years later
when he died for good, they knew it was only
temporary, a requiem having everything to do
with the earth, its profuse and barren times,
the burial diminished by the earlier
God-filled rising.

This morning I see you
without seeing your awful death; a brother with two sisters

brought together from our separate places
brimming with laughter and dance, because at times we danced.
Seven years, two thousand and some odd
miles away, we celebrate, running
on the anniversary of the night our mother
told the doctor she wanted to die instead of
get you born. This time you come in the day's
bright honor. This time, hallelujah,
we close the book, we give our promises
to the living, we hold up the sign of ourselves
like the sun held up to the face of this life.
And all the past lies down for the ordinary
and triumphant scene on this one morning
like a peridot to dispel the terrors of night,
for the road your body takes, still unburied.
And we rise, unburdened, all of us who believe
you are alive, not dead at twenty-six in D'Arbonne, Louisiana.

THE FAITHFUL

In the hierarchy of things to see, the larger
stones come last, then the moss or lichen covered
near water, and the routine
glide of minor birds in the path of vision.
Because the eye's accuracy is approximate,
squirrels weigh less than rabbits. And because we like
what disappears, deer count most, though foxes
bring a certain gift if accidentally
glimpsed at sunrise in an open field.
Deer on the road at night mean to tell you
something's lost: my embryonic first child
did not survive the omen of a five-point buck
crossing the midnight road before us. And though I slept,
head in my husband's lap the rest of the way home,
we would be split forever by our ways
of seeing that grief.

What I grew up seeing as a wall of green
is really a thousand species of the rare
and seldom seen. The average swamp
is a death of stumps and snakes
the eye teases from the submerged
vegetation, hardly knowing what's imagined
from what the brown water covers. So I look now
past the lie of broken cypresses,
the scum and sludge of those static limbs,

to swamp fishing with my silent mother,
night crawlers and the bag of macaroni at her feet.
I know she counted lucky our winters rich with fish
hovering in the water's buggy heat
and the accident of common need
that brought us to the birds.
Hunched over in the prow, brooding into dawn,
I saw them without attention: one generic white
as they gathered, an occasional red
detail on the crest of a neck.
What came exact were the bottom-eaters,
cat and bream, trash fish
whose bloody gills and writhing I still see
plain as day in the bottom of the boat.
She could wait for hours,
devoted to the hidden: a glimpse
of the nested blue-veined
eggs among the stink of the water hyacinths
catching at our boat, those fake orchids
buoyed up like bladders on their leaf stalks.

Now rounding a bend near an opening in the pines
where a mass of tiny buttercups
dot the weeds, I barely catch sight of
a dozen or so goldfinches darting up,
themselves like flowers someone has thrown.
That kind of seeing is enough
to keep me for a week. With other birds
even the names determine sight:
bittern and cormorant for their shyness
or the ghostly rattle of a kingfisher

making a certain claim on us in exchange
for visibility. I've tripped on the running path,
thinking folded leaves were wings,
and even what I don't witness can stop me cold:
evidence of a jay, jab by jab,
tearing to pieces a rose finch still in the nest.

But we disregard the penalty for seeing,
just as we think we see in birds
our own possibilities for grace;
our only touch is with tongue and teeth
in the syllables of their lovely names.
And because each one of us has flown in dreams
we dreamed perhaps just once, those wings for us
precede words, precede the logic
of how things rise. Some pinion
connects who we are with whatever pulls us
to walk into the evening's wetland grasses
in an air made of sounds we listen for,
a hearing that reveals what rises—
hoping for the scarlet ibis and the black-crowned,
that catalog of all the herons,
the grace of seeing that will save us.

FROM

Guardian

(1995)

BLUES: LATE AUGUST

Bluefish boil the water silver; they tangle in the chase
and the frantic smelt run headlong onto the sand,
caught by the blinding mirror, the water's

skimming sheet. And in the tide's remove, the knife-like
bodies hardly struggle, laid out in one long row
like silverware by a child's hand. All the bathers

scramble out of the sea, fearful of the indiscriminate
bluefish jaws, and around our heads, the gulls
flail about, sharp-eyed and diving, a frenzy

guarding the feast. All along, the ocean
turns its back to the spectacle, locked
in its usual resolve, but I can't move

for love of the world, its terror and sufficiency.

POEM FOR MARRIAGE

Pretend you have never been in love,
pretend that nothing has changed you,
that it is possible to live without violation.
You could go back to the girl you were
at fifteen, reading for hours in a kind of sleep,
angry to be awakened—the lives around you
never the emotional equal of those
you lived on the page. Those years
belonged to a loneliness you never questioned;
so complete, the sweet ache of the self
gazed back at you from the mirror
as if she were the stranger. Now if you wake alone,
it's only because the other is still sleeping.
At the edge of the Atlantic, you rise
in slow motion, needing to leave it all
undisturbed: the mutual plans and concerns,
the temporary obliteration of sex.
Exhilarated by the privacy and the light, you walk out
to the beach, and watching the tide play
its trick of distance, decide to go
to the land's farthest reach, that ghostly point
where the water's body joins the sky.
You walk fast and straight out, through shallow pools
becoming more frequent and deep until you sink
sometimes to the knee. Until there's more
empty water than sand and it is so clean

that nothing speaks of living; even the one
sea-rotted body of a man o'war is no more
than a marker your eye uses to keep perspective
on what's large, what's small. Looking back,
you can barely see the toy-sized house,
white on white in the haze: it has nothing
to do with you. Everything out here
has the holy cast of blue, everything is filled
with wind. And finally, the sand's last edge—
the entire ocean looms. How easy,
you think, to take one more step;
to walk until your legs flail and go useless,
your body washing forward, over and under
with its involuntary struggle, and you turn
from the confines of breath to a world
wholly imagined. . . . But love
has had its way with you; that tide pulls you back
to its fragmentary shore of loss and gain.
Until you are not yourself but part
of another story, as if your life were a child
crying for milk.

WHO KNOWS

where his tumor came from?
My husband wants to bury it
in the food we eat: wine or no wine,
what does it drink? The mysterious X and Y
of coupling and conception
swelled their way to pregnancies—
his headache, my nausea,
CAT scan, ultrasound,
our diagnoses. Can we trust
meditation and massage, the surgeon's
knife, the itch and burn
of stitches, or the work of scars?
Oh the products of our labor:
one in a jar left on a shelf for study,
the other we take home
in blue blankets. And what is it
that takes hold in the baby's
dream and brings him back, the long
siren cry of a baby fighting sleep?
Lower and lower he wails,
falling into dark, a rondo
slowing only to rise. What will satisfy
the little master? He pulls
at the unlikely breast, bluish drops
gleaming in his mouth, slack now;
finished in the crook of my arm,
the head lolls. Nothing else

can get milk out; my furious pumping
makes a poor ounce.
But how the baby fattens, little pear
thighs and such knees, such round
ineffectual feet. Maybe they make tumors too.
For that matter, what about the plum's
decaying fruit against the screen,
the seeds at the heart
of the tree's last apples,
vivid as pain in the appetite of snow—
white fists of too-early,
disfiguring snow.
Toppling in his fat suit
the eight-month-old gurgles.
Does all the dumb world know?
Maybe anything the shape of a head
knows, or any one of the body's eyes
where heaven-knows-what can get in.
Oh splinter, speck of affliction,
from where? Tiny, tiny, the god cell
wants to make brothers.
If you listen, it howls, ordinary life
with its quantum leap.
We turn in our beds, we turn and turn.

THE STORY

Innocent and earnest, good at marathons, the surgeon
believed in his hands; he said
he'd cut the tumor out, a convoluted and unnatural thing
wrapping its tentacles around the brain's little house.
Nothing more than architecture, he paused:
he knew about the maze, the puzzle.
He put on his white clothes; over his entire being
he laid white cloth. He gathered his men
and the one woman, and they all went in
with sharp instruments. The drill took the bone
and the red spray flew. They found the right room
in the back of the head. They found the tiny monster heart
wavering near the brain stem.
But no microscope could turn down the folds
of the pineal gland, where the soul looked out
its infinite window and saw the altered light.
Saw the giant hand that was not God's.
No scalding oil fell; the soul did not shiver
and hide its face. The light of science
went on burning, and so did the knife,
dismantling cell by cell. But the soul was calm.
It waited out the industrious nine-hour sleep,
dozing itself at times to avoid the blinding
overhead lamp. The soul sang its little songs,
dreamless infant songs: far beneath and years gone,
complementary to the Mozart the surgeon played.

Humming away, the soul wove a tuneless cover
for every memory of intrusion, fear, and pain.
And when you woke—
cut even where the clamps had held the mask to your face,
bandaged and swollen and clean,
changed but for the wide pacific blue of your eyes—
love still lay there: handsome, without innocence,
and utterly faithful.

SEVEN MONTHS

A slight infection of the ear,
then plain cold human will:
his whole body said no.
He stiffened in my arms, screamed
to see the nipple bared.
After two days of pumped milk and tears,
screamed even at the great white bra
when I unbuttoned my blouse.
Midnight came, and when he stirred
I sang, coaxed the baby
close, then as he fell to sleep,
tricked him with the gradual
transfer from bottle to body.
He shuddered, his lips moved
half-opened on my skin and he took back
the hard, veined breast
swollen as big as his head.
Pain was part of it; I ached
with relief as his clean taut pull
drew the arrows from my chest.
Then settled back in the rocker—
dim pinpoints of stars, moths
tapping the screen. Ordinary September.
But the little mouth was resolute:
last time, last time

went the rhythm of its suck.
What could I do
but give him up.

NOT WRITING

The world is indifferent—
who wants poetry but my own dark ego
setting words to its music.
Again it is night, the short day's end
with him, little child
banging against my brow, bruising
my lip with his hard gold head.
We are playing the mother game of rock, rock
forward and backward, till sleep
can take his quick body,
until I gaze on stillness: eyelashes and lips,
the slight transaction of breath.
My own eyes grow heavy,
heavier at the thought of my cluttered desk
in a far room. Oblivion,
is that what I want?
Not the orchestra and chorus
but the white rug, the folded wash,
the scrubbed porcelain sink.

THE GREAT QUIET

I have been dreaming about sleep,
eyes closed and snow
thick on the skylight.
And in the children's rooms
utter silence, only the sweet things
laid in their places and the brief order.
Nothing there but the practical
breath, the body governed by air.
No wonder I am called

away from my other life, the defining
self that admits nothing but the mind's
endless digging. I wake with a start,
fearing the moment
a child's breath falters and I am not there
to shake the body back,

while this hand drags over the page.
All I want is to sleep,
to rise before daybreak in the far room.
But what will you pay, the voice echoes

cold in the dream
where paper is piled against the window;
where my hair and skin have turned
to powder, and when I speak

to overtake the great quiet, to call back
my daughter, my son,
my throat is a long avenue of ice,
cutting the familiar good words
at their source.

MOTHER'S DAY, 1993: HEARING WE WILL BOMB BOSNIA

I have taken away every unsafe thing,
surrounded him with softness as he sleeps. But I have no way,
truly, to keep him unharmed, and knowing this,
I live with a certain condition, a swelling
in the complicated region of the chest.
It catches me unaware this lovely morning
as I drink my second cup of coffee
twenty minutes past his usual waking, resisting *what-if*,
reminding myself that he hardly slept last night.
I've learned what asthma can do: his blue face
when the airways close, dull shadows under his eyes.
Called from sleep, I've found him
sitting up, both hands braced against the wall.
I hold tight, his thin shoulders, trunk, hips
racked with coughing, every muscle and nerve
negotiating the art of breathing. And though
I've bought the machine that like magic
opens his tubes and restores the air, deep gulps
he takes in like a drug, and gives him back
to perfect sleep, every bizarre consequence
now comes rushing through, a risky wind in spring,
knife-like in the blossoming world.

And so I turn, horrified and hating
my cowardice, from the magazine, the cover photo

of the dead child. I can't look at the shrouded head,
the bloody mouth exposed and slack
above the brief, unchildlike clothing,
and below that, as if nothing were wrong,
the tender arc of the belly. Oh that familiar
part of the child a mother kisses.

RAPTOR

I make the mistake of telling him
about the stump just off the path to the beaver dam.
How in the canopy of hemlocks, the deer's
wintering ground, a great owl dragged down
dove after dove, leaving on his makeshift table
mats of feathers and thrown-up rubble,
the egg-shaped pellets of rib and skull.
He's got to go there, he pleads,
not happy with the three tail feathers I saved.
Death is deep in him, its pull
certain in the details of his play, the way
benign objects become guns and knives.
Let's be bad guys, his small voice quivers,
us and *them* rising out of the dark
I think now is fundamental.
But my son's not like some other children
you've heard about, the ones who hide
from their mothers, run laughing into the road.
Victor over every monster, he would never
leave his bed in the dead of night,
unbolt the door and let himself out
into the heavy snow. He wouldn't do that—
would he, wander, dreaming,
until the cold carried him away.

THE PERFECT SERVICE

The truth is, the child protects me, takes away
the obligation to be someone other than myself.
In the full-blown spring, his clumsy feet
hidden in the grass, his fat palms in the thick
clumps of narcissus, everything's naked.
The earth is full of openings: he might disappear
if I turn my back. Bees, blackflies, the endless teeming
world hovers around his flawless head.
It would go on existing—and what about me,
how could I face all this beauty in his absence?
The expectation of loss makes me crazy. Better to have
the cold, to walk out without dread in the deepening snow—
winter's breath affirming my own nature—
how firmly I fastened layer after layer on his small body.

EARTH

You see a woman of a certain age,
not old, yet seeing every sign
of how the world will age her.
More and more, you'll find her in the garden
but not for onions or potatoes.
She wants blooms, color,
a breaking in the earth's disorder.
Swollen branch, the right bird—
they can make her cry. And the fussing
over moving this or that to the right location.
Learning to be alone,
she brings out ten varieties of rose,
armed against pest or blight
and the cutting northern cold
she fights with blankets of dirt.
Earliest spring will find her hovering
over the waxy perfection of tulips, the ones
closest to the thawing ground.
You'd think it's the opening she loves,
the loosening flower revealing
the meticulous still-life deep in the cup.
But what she needs is to see
those stiff-petaled, utterly still ones
rise out of the dirt.

The weather won't cooperate. She sinks
hundreds of bulbs in the rain,

mud on her hands, black smear on her neck.
For this birthing, all she pays
is stiff joints, and she knows again
the insistence of flowering.
Falling, she knows the flowers
fall to the season, and the seasons
to the great wheel. Fallen, she's learned
to prefer the fallen.

FROM

What to Tip the Boatman?

(2001)

THE OWL

How far did she fly to find
this pristine town on the edge of winter?
Crows have set up their kingdom—
a yacking flock louder than traffic
maims the morning air.
Day sends the coven screaming
in pursuit, black rags
haggling from clump to clump

of the decorous elms and oaks.
The dog's mouth hangs.
I follow his gaze through the shudder
of limbs to the still source, the center
of their flapping. The barn owl
commands a branch, the crows scatter
and aim, cutting around her
placid weight, something more of earth

than air. She stares straight ahead
as if focused on something she alone
can hear, their outrage at who she is
no more than a furious snipping,
until in one motion, she heaves upward,
her body transformed by sky.
The crows gloat, their battering
closes her path, and she misses a beat,

stumbling in the air
like a silence disrupted. The crows'
fat riot, their *mine, mine, mine,*
rules the sky. Call the owl
sadness, the one who watches
from the other side.

OLD TRICK

Spring wants me back,
and I should know better than to heed
that old hag, the goddess
disguising herself with the first green
she can muster. Her true self hanging around,
gray, icy, bent, gazing from the corners
while I glory in the fine scribble
skimming the trees. I let her
bear the weight of my heart,
not my first mistake: every year she promises

to bring back what I love, and for awhile
she does—a flower here, another there,
fast-talking me through the price
I'll pay later. It's one panorama
followed by the next, the returning
birds in a parade, finches
twittering at dawn. They too

make you think you can trust them:
look at those nests, their faith
at your feeder, but I can tell you this,
keep an eye on the children.
September will come, the ripe business
whirring—everything
you can't see in all the greenery,

its constancy already tinged: a slight cast,
a whine. Your own girl will vanish
under that yellowing wing.

SOLSTICE

I.

The child, thirteen, pushing away
the clip that tamed her hair.
The child with a pistol against her ear.
In the great life of things, a small noise
against the noise of spring. So small,
the mother downstairs only heard
the sound of something falling.

2.

She went, young enough to believe
nothingness is an empty field—
so many blackbirds out there you couldn't see,
wings with their red and yellow bars. The one
clear note coming from somewhere, a nest
to settle in. Where she fell, a world
would rise to hold her.
Isn't that what the story teaches?

3.

They stumble in the yard, the parents
leading all the classmates
stunned around them. Just beyond the funeral
heat, a meadow burns in the glare,

the new hay pales.
Every parent invents a story.

4.

No one knew she wanted the dark, that girl
whispering into a book—
already a woman's tongue, an eye.
A last shake of her hair, and another world
took her words, the ground opened
for her bones. She's under the nursery-grown tree's
accomplished shape, a small fact fixed
between the pine and lilac.
She was young enough to want a home down there.
And the ghost you've heard for months now?
That's what failure sounds like,
explaining and explaining.

NOON

I.

What adolescent can bear her mother?
Her words, her touch. The baby
who hung to my ample thigh
veers away, whips her horse
to go faster. She's testing
this gelding; she'll have him
charging through the afternoon—her reckless will
aiming for that surge
in the chest, the swallow of romantic dark.

2.

Something's wrong. The day's brilliance
shakes the horse. His eyes whiten,
he throws his head—some command
bears down from the heaven
of sun-eaten blue. Circling, circling,
the girl uses what she knows:
leg grip, seat, the danger
of showing the horse her fear.
I can't stop him, her voice level
as they bolt past. The field's sod rips
and heaves, black ruts
open for the stumble.

All I can think is how calm she is,
caught in a race that promises
to send her flying. Now she's forward
in the saddle, willing to go
with what's been given.
Flushed, steady, her hands
hold quiet, cupping the reins
as she's been taught.

THAT YEAR

Winter nailed itself to the ground.
My girl was fourteen, breaking and freezing.
She'd slice another hole in her body,
not pierces but a ragged stitch
circling her arm.
March came, the bad snow
kibbled to rot. Dog-kicked, hungry days
ate at her; a red slash
streaked through her chopped hair.
More in bed than not,
she wanted her black room, the walls lined
with pictures: Cobain sprawled
dead in his Converse All-Stars, rabbits
tortured for eye makeup, the clubbed seal's fur.
Everywhere she looked: the unyielding world.
She rubbed her own cut fingers into the evidence
hanging there, the perfect smiles, anorexic
and bulimic, the baby in the toilet, the stalker.

Outside, I turned my back
to the prevailing weather, studied
my good preparations—gardens I'd planted
in last fall's rain. The weeks would come
in the order of snowdrops, crocuses,
daffodils, tulips. I'd planted according

to every specification, the good mother
charting soil and depth and food.
Everything in my rich dirt was sure to rise.

FOR MONTHS

I dragged out of my hard sleep,
dense with its journeys,
dreading the moment which returned me
to the stairs leading to her room.
I couldn't move, fearing
each step toward the evidence
of blades I kept taking away:
warned first by the walls,
not their writing forms, but colors
tipped with a drying red that told me
she'd found some new place on her body to hate.
I'd travel through her rage
to find her flung on the bed—lucky arrival
if all I saw were old signs
of cuts and bruises.

I'd wait. I had so far to go
in absolute stillness, dying
to hear some small sound of her breath,
an inhalation, a turn, her life
just resting. The hell of the place
had wormed itself inside me so deep
I couldn't climb out. The little self
closed up tight, refusing to speak
unless she woke—the bargain
that replaced every other.

WHITE PRIMER

Even the clock is a liar:
the clouds' blank ceiling
claims whatever light falls from the sky.
I wake to the day, an arrow
aiming for the hour to call the nurse,
caretaker of the new white world
where my daughter lives, all her color
stripped in the name of health.
Doesn't the snow come to let the earth live?
So too will they cover the girl with white,
all that raging blossom of the self.

Don't ask me to believe in this season.
White nametag, white gown, the red lesions
like roads going nowhere. Covered, you see,
by the weather of this place:
you will not, you will not, you will not

until she hears it like a heartbeat in the white tempest.
All passion spent, all will,
she is good enough for the allowed visit,
the allowed room. Led to her
I can't read the map of her cold face.
Nothing reveals the child I knew
but the hopeless tangle of her hair.

CUTLERY

You must earn the fork,
but only after you've earned
the spoon. All you'll know
of the knife
is the blade you remember,
cousin to the fork's five prongs,
those scissored lines
you dragged along your arm.
Points for the healing,
points to earn anything
hell-bent for damage.
Nothing's innocent, not
in this world. You'll eat
like the civilized only before
dismissal through the double
metal door. Ignore that bell
from the other side: the visitor
you'll have to earn as well.
You're the zero
on heaven's chart.
Nothing's for you
but this plate of white food.
Two fingertips and one thumb
will make a clever tool.
Hungry enough, you'll slave
to institutional hours.

It's twelve: you eat,
at one you'll speak.

Don't want to eat?
Don't want to speak?
We'll have to put you all alone
in the metal bed in the metal room
with all the metal lights
turned out. Pound,
and stirrups will hold you down.
Scream, and it's double
time, twice the fear
that makes you open up the scabs
in the Solitary Room, where you hear
the little voice of the one
that brought you,
the one that won't quit
breathing in your ear.

"AS IF MAD IS A DIRECTION, LIKE WEST . . ."

I'm caught in March, the humdrum
ice-snow-ice fusing to a single gray.
I live on the road, headache

reeling to backache, hospital
to home, nowhere hours, hinged
and strung to her string of hours

in an unmapped hell. Where's the lock,
thread to the ultimate
pattern-maker, puppet-master

of the wires that make her jump?
I navigate the rut, my numb feet
dance—on the brake, on the gas—

leaping the back-road curves. I'm
programmed in a moving blur,
mother emblem, a stick-figure

doll to the daughter who jerks
and cries. Bent behind the fixed wheel,
I'm a blond smile in a black car,

unstitched. She's got the needle.

THE RUIN

When I was young, it was enough
to save myself. Childhood's house gave way
to the birds of the night, the rich
Louisiana dark which in its green
carries melody and chorus.
I set my own clock to it, rising
to rain in leaves, a voice
that told me I could leave that place.
Even later, the sun reflecting the image
of water onto a bedroom ceiling
could wake me.

But when my daughter disappeared,
no beauty gave back a reason to live.
I was nothing but mother, I would blow out
the world's candle. No burning,
no fire with its regeneration,
not even ash, that little cold ruin.
It was then I understood
the nothingness of the sea,
the crush of waves driven across miles,
riptides and currents deepening
in a water too vast to freeze.
Thousands of feet, impenetrable:
no diver, no machine, could breathe
in the time it took to reach that bottom;

nothing could live in that black, the descending
zones that cancelled out creatures—
the tiniest slime of protoplasm, eggy scum
on the chalky mud, whatever design
managed to quiver three hundred fathoms down
to the zero of the final zone.
And everything above rendered trivial
by the great salt body rocking
through sea floor canyons and mountains.
All of it a locked tomb, and me
in my iron boat.

INTERMEDIARY

When she came back, my daughter
brought November's moonless nights,
hunters and frenzied deer,
gunfire over the hill—a world
exposed under the bare trees.
She heard the dogs, and didn't sleep.
And though I couldn't stay awake,
I wouldn't leave her room,
tea at my elbow, arms crossed
to prop me up. Vigilance was all I had,
unlike the hospital, the ones who taught her
to use what she knew, a medicine
in small doses; how to go back
and forth, traversing darkness
as if it were a footpath. It was hell to me,
watching from the other side
of the one-way glass. All I could hear
was the slight buzz of fluorescence,
the stainless walls guarding
her white skin. I couldn't touch
for fear of leaving some mark; my hands
might hold her back from the work
she had to do. They'd hardly let me visit.

I was no guardian. I never knew
what she knew, never followed

through the woods, down to the river,
the abandoned tracks running beside it,
useless steel in the litter and weeds.
Her new habits frightened me, her mouth
a stranger's, a tic in the pause
before she let herself speak, the healed
crosswork of cuts under the chiseled
blue stone that hung at her neck.
She'd found another mother, a faith
that pulled her from bed,
guided her across the swollen river
posted with warnings, where the trucks
loaded up the carcasses.
Cigarettes flickered, an oil fire
blazed in a drum, sign of the season,
and she waited there,
a knitted skullcap pulled low;
waited for the men, asking
How will you bless this?
How far can you carry this meat?

RECONCILED

Spectators on the field, we saw
the horse gallop toward us,
froth whitening his face: no rider.
She darted out as if he'd called her.
Fighting past his weave and lunge,
she caught his neck as he reared, the reins
leaping past one hand, the other
scrambling for balance; her feet
in a dance with his digging hooves.
Somehow she grabbed and clutched—
when he felt the pull, he bucked
to break away, climbed the air
intending to drag her, but she tightened
with all her being
the black leather bounds in her fist.
No girl's strength could hold him,
nothing explains why he turned back to her,
stunned and waiting.

AFTER PERSEPHONE

Heaven got sweeter, its paperweight curve
star-crazy at its purple center.
She'd found a god, a weapon in the works.
Something I hadn't noticed in the field
fought out of the layers and took her.
I tore away the land's every color,
withered the smallest grasses. Every heartbeat
went blank, I dismantled the ticking.

They only say what I took, not what I gave:
roots and strong light, glory
in the single shoot, green currency
of the just-born. From the irredeemable,
the buried—this is how a self gets made.
Remember, that darkness contained the seed
sealed in the swollen red globe.
Hell had to pay.

WHAT TO TIP THE BOATMAN?

Delicate—the way at three she touched
her hands tip to tip, each finger a rib
framing the tepee of her hands.
So tentative that joining, taking
tender hold of her body, as if the ballast
of her selfhood rested there. Already
she could thread tiny beads through the eye
and onto string, correctly placing each letter of her name, sorting
thin black lines to make an alphabet,
the needle just so. She loved that necklace less
than cat's cradle, a game to weave
the strand through forefinger, ring finger, pinkie.
She could lace a basket, a boat
that could even carry water. *What to tip
the boatman?* I asked, trying to amuse her
with church and steeple turned to my empty palm.
Naptime, she'd lie there making shapes
above her, signing the air.

Later I saw the light touch in those twinned
fingertips had become her way
of holding still, keeping balance.
She had reached home before I did, finding
no mother at the bus stop, and entered
the silenced house for the first time alone.
Ancient, venerable, the whole place

waited, a relative with smells and creaks
she hesitated to greet. When I found her
she had made her way to the formal great room,
polite center of the hectic house where even
the clock's old thud gave back the heart
of simple waiting. Good guest, shadow
on the rose Victorian settee, she sat,
her hands precise before her, an offering.

THE RETURN

You magic thing, you brother,
erupting from underneath,
swallowing up whatever you wish.
Not enough to own everything below
this ground I govern—no,
you with your kingdom of rocks
took my one uncut jewel.
Something new to turn this way and that
on your throne down there.
Now she's eaten the earth's seeds,
you have to give her up. She'll be back,
but never with that innocence
you wanted.

We'll both have her, but it's nothing
more than a bargain she's bound to keep.
She's carved a self now—not for you or me.
Look how carefully, gleaming in the light,
she rows herself out.

PERSEPHONE, ANSWERING

The girl in me died.
I watched her go under. In time
I turned back, answering the world
with my dead weight.
I entered the delirious air,
a spring I could make nothing of.

The question is
what is the end of grief?
I knew my mother then
for the first time: the bright self
withers, the soul
whitening like a stem that can't push its way
through rotted leaves, no balmy light
to fatten it into love

—if blooming is what we think is love.
Mother made herself into a bitter root,
living for a few days of flowering.
What art is that, always holding on?

DEMETER THE PILGRIM

She took the guise of crone,
black robes, gaunt face reflecting
the agony that had brought her
to the sisters at the well. She was searching,
crying, reduced from goddess
to one with an arm outstretched.
Even human pity would do, a human child.
For aren't all babies alike
in their physical, grasping selves,
their unmediated need?

A hurricane, a famine.
Who could deny the weather, the iron ocean
rocking, the fear they all would break
in the end. An old woman—
who wouldn't take her in?

She made herself useful, tending
the hearth, the infant who had learned
to babble and reach. When she took him
in her arms, head against her breast,
all the green world washed over her,
smell and touch returned to the source.

You know the story. We've passed it down,
a token in the gray landscape, a winter

you make your own. Once again,
it's not so much the actual moment
the girl is snatched away, but the watching,
time waiting with its noose,
all your terror balanced there.
And the future
slides out like the fog offshore,
its own continent
floating between the sea and sky.

FIGURE OF FORMAL LOSS: PEARL

No longer someone's mother,
she's still a woman, doing the usual chores.
Now she's bending over melons, a fragrant
pile in the grocery store. And there it is:
gold, swollen to its ultimate
paleness, a great globe, the skin so thinned
and stretched against the heavy flesh
she can almost see through it. The blossom end
with its slight bulge, almost the soft spot
on a baby's head—she can imagine a pulse
in the fruit. Bending there, caught in the luxury
of choosing among so many lovelinesses, she
doesn't know her own rapt face. She's moved back
to the sea, transported there, reminded
of the outline barely discernible in the low fog's
nothingness, wet gray cast over the morning.
She's walking through it again, drifting forward,
following the white line the water makes,
the thread of continuity that keeps her moving.
How far can she walk this way, how long
can stasis define the available heavens,
the miles of beach she thought she knew?

She thinks of the sun out there, the gold ball
suspended over the eastern sea, and then her own
dull settling of densities, the cold veil she wears—
how can any light ever break through?

Now with melons, in the middle of an ordinary morning,
this happens: the sea and its obscured sun
brought back whole, and she is swallowing hard
to keep hold of a moment that has somehow
moved her beyond acceptance,
passing through all suffering to the core.
Not willed or understood, not some mood
traversing the surfaces of self, a temporary
easing of the burden. No, it's as if
her dead child has curled into some accommodating
spirit, an abiding that settles into its own place.
The child curled on her side, sleeping
as children sleep, bound up like a fist, turned inward
as if to protect. A grain, a speck, so insistent
that the self forms its layers around it
one thickness at a time, at first gray, the sullen
lubricant accruing, and as it grows, hardening,
taking on a luster, a lightening of the mineral.
Until, degree by degree, every sorrow goes pure,
brightening its coat, still forming itself
over the kernel of the child who is not
so much the child she made inside her, but her own
particle of self. The child as a figure of formal loss,
and over it, the luminous shell of her own being:
a shining that passes for who she is.

FIST

The master talks about a life,
how it goes on building
dead coral, leaving something beautiful,
but this is not the way of children.
No, they take their lives elsewhere,
into thin air. The lost, the saved,
either way they disappear, their shapes
changing so intently that you come
back to them the way you revisit
a beloved shore, the mile of beach you'd known
like your own palm. This landmark
or that, shells coveted
for their rimmed blue—these pull you back,
but winters have passed. Did you only imagine

their brief, early bodies? Their fat hands
with the submerged knuckles, tender
indentations at the base of each finger,
each dot a marker for the bone
the weather of years would uncover.
Underneath that sweet fat, a future
composed itself, wintered and grew lean:
taught the hand to make itself a tool,
hold the toy, the spoon. And later, the knife,
the razor, the gun: instruments turned
against the self. A self grown by then

remote, rigid, unwilling to come back
to you, who nursed that body.

Remember the first months you tended it,
hour by hour; the years you checked it
sleeping, naptime and nighttime,
leaning over the breath's tide as if you
could trace it back to its start:
the rush of water, the rude air
invading the infant lungs, the gasp
which changed everything. Remember
the first time you unfurled
the tight fists, the initial strength
given the baby to save herself.

FROM

White Sea

(2005)

SALT

All those years I went the way of grief,
  turning my stony eye on disorder, something to be cleaned
    and fixed. I was lost, scrubbing away at the hidden,

hating the vase where the fruit flies nested,
  the artful bowl that held ruined fruit.
    Throw away the rot, I said, making myself saint

of the immaculate, not knowing a thing about the soul.
  Meanwhile, little spirit, essence, psyche, anima,
    the forever-alive but-unpinnable one

turned its gaze away, claimed a crack,
  found a rusty needle, curled up in the eye of it.
    In the pine floors alone, a million crevices,

a million particles of grit, pinch, and crumb.
  What sea in my bucket could wash the world clean?
    And who knew the soul

was right at home in dust, passing
  through every incarnation: the tiny breathing
    mite it entered in the gray swirl under the stove,

expelling itself into a draft that carried it
  into the filmy grease so lightly pocked
    on the cabinet glass. Releasing, floating down,

the soul finding the one grain of salt
　　lying there under my nose. Me at the sink,
　　　　scouring the porcelain, not seeing.

THE OLD QUESTION

What will it take to let myself speak?
June is a chorus of blues, delphiniums
rioting at the gate, the pressing
summer air. On the deck, lemon birds
quick as poppy seed, chime
and spring into the morning blaze.
It's too clean, too clear, this weather

set against my fear. Cornered,
the old question screeches and dives.
Tell the truth, I think, and what is that
but a creature with claws?
I bite my lip, remembering
last evening's walk at the deep end of dusk
when everything had shut itself up
but the one yellow-eyed, secretive thrush—
silver call in the night.

THE SOURCE

Morning arrives in Louisiana, green going sour
with heat. Against the screen, oleander
scrapes its thicket of blooms,

cardinals gather in the yard, too many to count
with their rough voices, the single abrupt chirp.
My grandfather will not touch those birds,

though he shoots others with a stone and sling
and stews them whole,
nested in onion broth with whole garlic and clove.

Plain brown wrens, song sparrows—for him
no different from the figs he picks into his hat.
I hide in the muscadine vines

pretending to play. He can't speak English
and I won't speak Greek. I can hear him calling,
each word hitting its mark,

and so I go to him with all my refusal.
From the blushing spot on each blossom end,
he peels back the skin for the fig's red meat,

he slips the coarse black covers off the grapes
and feeds me in the shade. It's too hot.
I lick the skin on my forearm. He's talking,

telling me that taste is like the sea.
I have never seen the sea. He's in another country
trying to tell me something. I look away.

THE WAITING

Not my climbers: black gum, sour gum, oak,
not the silvery underside of the dear mimosa
where I spent hours reading, but Louisiana's tree,

green through every season. Under the magnolia,
on my back, knees bent, bare feet flat on the dirt,
I gazed at my hands, already my own—

in them a dream of myself, my on-going-ness—
as if the future were caught in the outspread
web of my fingers. Their admirable length, their span

already a piano octave, seemed more than a child's,
mattered more than the silly girl in school
who questioned my color. When I held up my splayed hand,

light shone through the outline, pink skin
back-lit, just as the light lit each leaf,
the precise stems radiating outward from the branches

which surrounded the trunk. Exactly spaced,
they allowed only pieces of sky, the path of white buds
sensibly wound, not yet heady with scent

in the demanding heat. The day's fleshy blossoms unfastened
cupped petals large as dinner plates, their perfection
poised and unassailable. Just to touch them

meant a bruise, a yellow-brown shadow on the cream.
What I owned was the dim ground, the secret
pathways for ants and beetles. The line of roly-polies

turned their thin bodies into BBs, metal balls rolling away.
Molding the damp earth around my fist,
I still made houses for toads, a walled village.

Poison was everywhere: snakes, the oleander
lining the house, where black folks left us okra or peas,
a bushel of something, at night

when no one knew they came. But for the time being
I could still turn away. The tree,
another gorgeous southern thing, held me

from a longing so fierce I would go numb with it.
That world outside would claim me, close the self, lock it tight,
and what would it take to open again?

CATALPA

My body woke whole and strong. The wings
came out of nowhere, joined me to the birds'
swoop and dive above the sunken land.
I could see the rim of watermark around each tree—
in the one recurring flight, catalpa trees
and Genie Bell's house just beyond.

We collected worms from the ruts of trunks or as they hung
like stamens of the long white flowers the trees put out
each June. All around was the nasty smell
of last year's leaves crushed underfoot, but in my double life
she and I flew above all that, above the entire grove
planted for fishing bait. The pasty gutsy worms
loved by perch and bass, sold up on the corner.
The bait for her Sunday fish.

On the bogged edge of D'Arbonne Pond
filmed with greenest-green, where the bottom-eaters doze,
I'd see her with the others, black faces
above the brimmed line of flowered dresses and hats,
bamboo poles arcing pale lines over the notched water. Quiet—
not like us on the manicured shore with our picnics and balls.
This scene is real, I think. Sometimes I confuse them,

the dream, that is, and the actual fishing.
I know the grove of catalpa trees from nights

I sort and piece. She bore me up on her wide body—
in that strange light she shone. We were safe up there,
I never doubted. I thought we all shared some secret something
in my blood, in my slow white half-breed blood.

CANE

When the mule balked, he hit him
sometimes with the flat of a hand
upside the head; more often
the stick he carried did its angry trick.
The mule's job was to power the press,
iron on iron that wrung the sugar
out of cane, circling under the coarse
beam attached to his shoulders and neck.
That mule of my childhood
went round and round. He made himself
the splintered hand of a clock, the groan
and squeak of machinery chewing
the reedy stalks to pulp, each second
delivering another sweet thin drop
into the black pot at the center.

He hit him with a rag, old headrag,
but the animal winced only with the thrash
of a cane stalk itself—he squinted
under the rule of that bamboo.
The sun was another caning, that burning
slow as the blackstrap syrup the boiled sugar made,
so true to the circle he dragged
we hardly saw him. We loved the rustling
house of green cane, blind in that field
of tropical grasses whose white plumes

announced the long season's wait.
We yearned for the six-foot stem, the eventual
six pieces the machete sliced
at the joints, then the woody exterior
peeled back lengthwise with a blade.
It was a black hand we waited for, his job
to lay bare the grainy fiber we chewed.
That juice on our tongues
was his sweetness at work.
Chester was his name, he kept the mule.

BURIAL

Later he died, and it was then I think
I began to give sense to every motion
I had not heeded. Already I could no longer
kill an ant, a wasp, without some smallness
setting in: the burden of my own hunger
apparent in every living thing. But that was after

Chester buried the dog, after he walked us down
into the swampy woods. Sunday morning, already October,
the grasses shot through with yellow, the locust
bearing its alligator bark. So early
we were in our nightgowns, my sister and I,
my brother trailing. The durable creatures of the air

zoomed and crossed, my heart lit with grief
for the dog, my own dear fierce animal
mysteriously dead, firing the rage which would lead me,
while Chester shouldered the dog on one side, the shovel
like a rifle on the other, come once again
as a favor to my mother, who had no man for this weight.

And the new sun faced us, flat across the flat land,
making its way across his quiet face
as he dug the hole. My sister sobbed, my brother watched,
and I was so busy in my head, even now
I can see only the lovely patterned fur
arranged in the hollow of red dirt. Not Chester,

who was one more thing in the landscape, his presence
something I took in like air. Not his glistening
onyx self, his color smooth as mineral, or the comfort
of the low voice giving a few words in praise of dog,
although I heard him take one deep breath,
the *amen,* when he finally rested.

WANT

Every sign of the day flies white,
throws the pump bucket and water jug,
covers the saw and screech of making do.
I come back to paper scattered on sand, shutters banging,

and my young self still out there,
stumbling on the blowing beach,
high tide sucking her ankles
as she fights her way in a sideways gust.

I can't see her through the storm
of so many years, and what can I do with her anyway?
Furious girl, daring it all
to get what she wants. So much wanting it's turned

indistinct, *silvery as the promise of torn clouds.*
As usual, she's all image and hyperbole. The hypnotic
sea foam churns up—what else?—beauty,
not the bitter brine of the hard water

slapped white. The fool in her
summoning Icarus caught up in pristine light,
and in the shattered sea, some miraculous
rising. She'll choke in the water's squall.

Midnight and my young self
will come dragging in, spent and bruised,
banging at the shack. The flimsy piece of driftwood
nailed to make a simple lever
                              will not hold the door.

MOONSNAIL

I killed it for its shell, its design and shape,
not caring about the animal coiled inside, faceless
mudworm, intestinal, with its amorphous foot
fixed like a door to repel crabs or gulls.
I thought I'd see some taut muscle, not that oozing,
the giving over of a thick pulsing jelly
wound and wound to its end. I didn't think of it
answering to a clock, hurling forward as the waves

shoved onto sand, waiting to open and burrow,
to feed before the water dragged it back.
Traffic of the tides, that ugly life
filled a house which took on hues of blue and rose,
some pretty moss as it aged, perfect form
spiraling to the innermost point
marked by a round black eye.

Five shells now, lined up by size,
but not like Russian dolls, an amusing emptiness
to fit a pattern. These are freed from their true selves—
the disgusting, the lax—though I admit, not evil,
not what my grandmother warned against: the devil
waiting for the opening praise provides.
Spit, she said, in the face of beauty or truth
to chase harm away.
                    It's useless to spit in this ocean,

always the churning surface and everything underneath
riding in. Polished by the sea's punishing thrust,
empty shells survive. But I didn't want those—
I chose the inhabited, the *something there*,
and removed it. It's simple: I laid each one out
in the blinding day, the sun did its work, the ants came,
then I shook it hard.

DEATH OF A GULL

Worse than his pain was his acceptance,
the wing loosely dragging beside him
while he did his best not to notice. As if the impossibility
might drop away, he ambled, a hen's shuffle
from oceanside toward the plovers' nesting ground,
but the little birds came diving, driving him back.
Beak open, he hissed like a swan, his only show.
Another gull glided down, just one—perhaps his mate—
companions side by side until he ignored
the cues for flight. She spiraled out of the path
of passersby, but he only turned his head away,
like a toddler's shy aside, to make the intruder disappear.

Day and night turned over, the waves
close then far. The weight dangling at his side
grew heavier and he learned to fix his eye
on the middle distance. Alone and offered up,
he roosted there, suffering the tide-rich sand
and the roving metal-throated birds
from which he once stole fish. The spewing waves,
the crabs awash, haphazard heads and claws,
offered nothing he wanted to eat.
The whole thing reeked. Overhead, the hypnotic
sequined blue glittered and teased.

The green sea went about its business,
sifting, hooking, grinding. Bottom waters
boiled and rose, feeding all the frenzied
multiplying cells, which brought the little fish,
the bigger fish, and then the seal,
whose lackadaisical tossing off of bones
made him the birds' life of the party.
The crippled gull heard them all, but as if
he lived in another country. There was nothing
but the square of sand he squatted on.
Flying was a prick of recognition gone foreign,
then a nagging absence, swallowed up by the wind.
Hour by hour, he became that emptiness,
just a breathing thing on the moving sand.
And then the line dividing the pulse
from the intake of air,
air ruffling feathers he no longer felt.

SPEECH TO THE SELF

People have been dying and you
are lying on the beach. You're lying here
listening to the world
inside: no, it's the soul in you,
and you want enough room to hear.
You lay down your bushy head with all that gray
flying out on the damp sand.
You let your head be its own weight, a rock
among all the other rocks on the stony
two or three feet of tide line—
the fertile wrack of it
made from dead things
and the miniscule cells they feed.

You fish for it, the tiny tail of a moment,
the trail end of a thought, a listening
you've ignored all this time. You think
I could make something with that, and
in that *maybe,* all possibility in you
becomes very still, your body
inert on the sand. Because all the dead ones
are living there too, guests
in the shell of a thought, and if it were real,
this shell would be a spiral shape,
a moon snail—oh but why bring the moon into it?
What did the moon ever do for you,

that preoccupied mother
nursing her schedule, half-here, flirting
half-light through mists and trees and buildings.
The soul doesn't want her moody truth.
Try on death for truth: the incomparable
here now, gone tomorrow.

Was it grief that sent your soul away?
To what secret room, through which stubborn door?
On the other side, she's inching her way out,
uncurling with the loosened thought,
murmuring in a breath. And you want
just to pull her out of there,
give her your voice box, like a toy,
a puzzle, the child in her
turning it over and over, putting it to her ear,
her small fingers probing in the flat light
until satisfied, she wakes to your waiting—
she has something to say.

THE RELEASE

I.

I lose myself in all the falling
leafy light, gold on gold
bartering through the afternoon.
How many leaves will it take
to fill this pond, where thousands float,
feathery, slight, gilding
the surface. The water has settled
into clarity, all its complication
brooding on the bottom, reminding me

of Linda near the end. She waited
as if waiting were the reason for it all,
oblivious to the bedside comings and goings.
Flickering with morphine, the face we knew
receded. She was feeding a great privacy,
moving past the years she once said
were fixed with our names;
moving past the self's accumulation
to the very point of spirit, dot
in the web binding our lives to hers,
drawn in and borne away.

The sky goes flat and all the forest
racket suspends. Bruised reds

interrupt the golds. I see the bird reflected
before I see the bird himself: the unfolding
heron's blue clockwork.
The water gives a shiver of disorder,
no more than a pause in a string of words.
A wasp lumbers in the air
with no screen to beat against.

II.

The field has been waiting all this time
    to offer up its green to bristle and bur,

the raspy wire hooking my ankle.
    I've needed to see these crossed grasses

flung by the mower, the nested feathers
    she could name. She knew every cricket and cicada

crowding the air. Doesn't that universe of keening
    make September a grieving thing? But as I reach

the trees' blind opening, a deer
    flies at me, wild-faced, the raised body

hurling itself forward, hooves
    veering as I freeze. And just like that, she's gone—

Linda, who I can't keep,
    even the rising trill of her laugh

already revised, reordered.
  The weather bears down.

I'm turned by the rush of sudden birds,
  a fan opening.

III.

We'll call this dying: the soul
fumbles out of the dark room into the darker
hallway, almost feeling its way as it separates
from the body's time and space.
It has to regain itself, this soul, its definition
caught as it has been for so long
in the body on the bed. The gorgeous quiet
has already descended, no hum or tick
or expectant sleep of a soul deeply tuned.
Maybe someone sobs, the guest
holds back, or the one
loved beyond all estimation still
holds the weighted hand. Or it is three a.m.
and whoever has lain beside the dying
all night with the work of waiting
walks out in pajamas into the black wet grass. . . .
But never mind, here's the moment,
almost with the last heartbeat: the soul
is stretching, hesitating forward,
a second of air, a brief exhalation of nothing,
more the shiver a little breath makes.
Then the pause in which something
is thinking itself forward

toward a distant twin, maybe a line of light
under the door that leads through the house,
then out into the night. Out to the celestial
shimmer that belongs to the earthly moon,
that appropriated body we believe
informs our own. And to the surrounding
kin of stars, star from dying star
passing on its dust, every physicality connected
to another in that transforming that keeps making
something of itself over and over again—yes, well,
imagine joy, as the soul gives it all
a brief nod and flies on past.

WHITE MORNING

How could it be so ruined, the woods
ravished by a grainy sleet, a gravelly white
sodden leaves and limbs poke through.
I have lost my killer instinct
for beauty, for embellishing and relishing
the art of it. No lacework to imagine
here: the spoiled autumn
dies into slush, and the deer who roamed free
yesterday, the thrill of my gaze locking theirs,
have quit the neighborhood. Not one captured thing
to trade, though I look hard
first one way into the wasted repetition,
then the other, but no, I cannot
coax a quarrel out of this unforgiving ground.

YOU MUST CROSS THE BLACK RIVER

If only is your governing rule,
each day's measuring stick held out
to find the lack, the thwart, the missing
you continue to mourn.

Poor heart, with its struggle and stutter,
its fat blue beating. And how could you
forget it—listening all night, head on your arm.
That voice in a knocking house

has nothing to do with the soul, what you call
unquenchable, bloodless
in the sweep of white. You break open the fruit,
the mass of swollen seeds, each its own

fiery globe, a ruby-flicker in the nested
chambers of pale flesh, for a glimpse
of *what-passes*. But even this holds you
to the physical, the mapped, and you must leave all that:

you must cross the black river
and take up the laws of nothingness and waiting.
She'll come, the one dressed cold and still
in a clamor of light.

PRAISE HIM

Dog whose middle name is *do good*,
whose sigh is the birth of patience; dog
whose middle name is angel, offering
the blessing of his lick, his weight as guide.
Carrying is what he does best, and so he does

love the stuffed bear we call Baby and all the risk
of teeth in fur, our captured hands as we grab
the sticks of the world, where he turns
his desire to even the inferior, insignificant
breaking ones. He holds them all, as he tries

to hold the low wind's message in his upheld nose.
He holds himself as guard, ears pricked
for the snow's command. Ice-crystals in his lashes,
eyes narrowing at the moon traveling under the cloud,
he'll burrow into the snow if it's too cold,

just as he finds the girl's side when she cries,
leaning his body against hers, finding
her eyes to hold, his eyes of the ever-present
mother, the language of *now* in his hungry tongue.
He knows with what degree of whine to shade

his answering bark; has learned to soften it
to a vowel when she questions, though finally

he must lie down with the secrets he carries,
heaving his weight aside, cornered in the one life
of the dumb, the never-to-speak, full with knowing.

SOUL

It is not the angel riding a goat,
trying to make him go. It does no work
with refusal or guilt, which loves
only its contorted self. But fancies instead
my terrier's long pink tongue,
how it teases out the bone's marrow,
tasting with all its muscle.

The angel is silver, but so is the goat
and the box on which they perch,
a Victorian gesture in the mansion
where I spent the fall. They have followed
me home, their permanent shine presuming,
while around me, everything withered,
slowly froze, and began its turn
toward white. The snow
is nothing but a great emptiness,
and I'm tired of trying to find a secret there.
But look—one leaf
skittering across the glazed surface
catches its stem to stand upright,
the shape of a hand waving.

FROM

Book of Dog

(2012)

CANIS

It was a small comment, wasn't it, about who they were
—that last year on the dunes when all the town talk
was of coyotes, prairie wolf in search of an ocean,

those footprints instead of rabbits' surrounding the shack
or half-sunk in the cranberry bog
just off the path. They heard the howling somewhere

behind their backs as they walked out past midnight,
singing at the top of their lungs:
abandon me, oh careless love—although they knew

the coyotes knew exactly where they were. No surprise
to either of them when they wailed unusually close
and loud on a moonless night after an argument,

this time a mean one about the dogs. For God's sake,
the dogs, how much trouble they were to him,
their feeding and whining and constant

need to go out, no matter how wet or cold. And on and on
till silence set itself between them, holding stiff
as each turned away to bed. But the coyotes just outside

started up their merciless lament, as if
the entire genus called them, had bound the tribe together
in protest for their brothers. Hours they heard the keening,

both of them sleepless, that rising, falling
complaint in their ears—until he couldn't bear it, he said
I'm sorry, I can't do this anymore, and she in a rush

of understanding the exact suffering fit of it, jumped up
and closed the offending one window's
half-inch crack, and just like that

in the dead center of a moan, the coyotes
stopped their noise; what I mean to say is
the wind stopped making that heartbroken sound.

ANTS WANT MY YELLOW MOTH

The one that came to me out of the sea, perfect
serrated edges of its six wings,
each seamless with tiny yellow feathers,
the two bright center ones with fake black eyes
pretending sight. Even drowned,
the wings held tight, a simple knot at the top
attaching them to the black worm of the body.
What fragile stitchery the tide held up,
carrying it in on a wave. I took it to my desk,
arranged it so as to see the colors as they dried,
the veins rising, shuddering with my breath.

But now, this ant has found its way
under my immaculate shack and climbed the pilings,
through gaps in the floorboards to one leg
of my writing table, and up that to the surface
plane of three cracked boards, where it scurries
to the moth: my creature.
Pulled from the sea with my own hands—mine, I think,
because I believe my very will can save it.

SONG OF IF-ONLY

If only the bird had been alive, not something dead
delivered onto sand; and not this packed cold sand,
where nothing moves even slightly, no blow-holes,
no scurrying things, and if only the shore birds'
seaweed nest, that little piping, hadn't been smothered
by a freak spring tide. Now the plovers must begin again:
eggs and hatching, the mothers' fake writhing
when they see me, squawking and dragging their wings
to save their chicks. Oh save me

from the whole painstaking work of early June—
this blowing fifty degrees, no sand bed of heat
in some dune bowl's hollow, no love,
and on this outer beach Euphoria
just the name of the shack I want in this driving rain.
And if only it would stop, shut itself up for good—
this off-key *if only* that goes on singing,
like some deranged child, repeating.

THEIR CHAMBER

She was thinking of his explanation
as a kind of Möbius strip, circling
endlessly, seamlessly reversing and twisting
to reveal the underside, on-going words. Lost in it,
she reached down into the limited
rough space between the bed and the wall,
and her hand came up skinned, the top layer
from knuckle to wrist peeled away.
This was part of her usual vigilance—
he would spill something, lose something, and she'd
rush to wipe away, find the missing,
like this automatic retrieving of his sock—

Beaded with blood, she examined
the wide scrape in addition
to sunspots, moles, the wormy down-under,
raised-vein look of her skin. Another thing on her body
to heal outside, while inside
running through her, the ribbon of his words:
no, then *yes, yes*, and *no* again. Oh what did he want

and how could she manage to wait
for the circling to stop—
how could she keep still.

ESSENTIAL TREMOR

More white tendrils to free
from rotten snow and the clenched ground—
tulips you hope that time will turn green.
You claw the drifts

till your gloved fingers freeze.
You wonder what fat grubs might tend them,
what hatching consume them?

Anxiety has forged another weather.
You wake with the shakes,
a waver when you stand, a slipstream
of early light propelling you
out to the garden.

What a grip has got you,
what a prison.

IN LENT

Dead deer a week now by the snowy gate.
Do I have to watch it be eaten? Do I have to see
who comes first, who quarrels, who stays?

And there is the question of the night,
what flesh preferred by which creature—
what sinew and fat, the organs, the eyes.

These appetites: it's enough
to know the swoop and cut of wings
over the snarl of something leaping away.

Do I have to see the icy figure fused to the ground,
scrabbled snow, not lovely or deep,
but the surface of something spoiled?

By now the rib bones arch over it all,
unbroken light shining between them,
above the black cavity.

And I hear the crows, complaint, complaint
splitting the morning, hunched over the skull.
They know their offices.

INTERSTICE

1. Between Grief and Sorrow

Grief staggers around the house
some thief has emptied.
It wants to tell me everything
all over again; blame is the story
grief hammers, hammering until my leg shakes,
my right foot won't stop tapping.
It's a dance for the shaken,
strung out with waiting, and now look
who's back to guard the door:
grief's half sister, dread.

2. The Coldest Weather

Young trees bend, white trunks slender enough
to spring back, softening the woods however they stand.
But in the bigger ones, you can hear
ice exacting its pull in the pines and spruce.
A pause, a sharp crack
and they snap, the whole tree
breaking away from the heartwood,
long tears of sapwood
going to pieces as they fall. Violent and brutal,
that was our winter. The ground deepened with waste.

3. In the Woods

Because there were no words he could hear,
I made myself mute, and because
the binding ice of another year

held the same branches down, they were dying,
and trying to free whatever green ones I could
was pointless. Still, I choose this task

for what it says about hiding and watching:
pulling at a dead limb releases a clatter,
and as I stand there,

dark surrounding trunks come alive
and leap away. The deer
is designed to resemble a tree,

and I only need take one brittle stick
to brittle bark and bang it to see everything plain—
the deer tearing through woods,

believing he is running for his life.

NOISE

We'd come so far, I kept saying.
I was full of myth, which is to say
full of an idea. The sea lent its own persuasion,
banging its way in. Listen, I said,
flying my music of need and want
into the far-reaching sky.

But inside that artifice
there was shoving, and he saw it.
He lay down and closed his eyes.
In the sand's obliging hollow, an anodyne
in the shadow's varying whites,
he made himself flat
so as to bring the warm sun against the plane of his body.
The demanding wind would pass right over.

BOOK OF DOG

1.

All praise to the light on the wing
of the wasp fallen to the wood floor,
enough universe for the dog
waiting while you are away.
But as long as your body sits on the chair,
he's not worried
where you are and when you look up
from that far place, he returns
may I lick your hand—the sign
you give back in the glory
song of the one word:
his name in your mouth.

2.

The other one's roaming closer, a shy dog
after this morning's rudeness,
belly to the floor, head bent,
she's crawling
to your chair, remembering
not to bark. Does my breath still stink,
can I sleep in your bed? What if
I promise not to wake you,

rolling over scratching an itch.
Thump goes the tail on the wood floor.

Bless her everlasting guilt.
Bless her eye on you.

3.

In the book of dog, a few syllables contain the world,
and you own them. You dole out *car, home, sit,*
stay—for the sweet yelp, the whine.
But at *cookie,* the wet mouth seizes,
the low growl transforming *give it to me*
into *see how I love you.* The pure
love we assign when the dog gets
what it wants. And when it doesn't,
that famously humble and contrived
looking the other way, studying the air,
the mote in the air—
the not wanting for anything, not saying
oh you dear one with the meat, the bone, the biscuit,
come back, give it to me.

4.

Again the wolf before I wake.
I am walking near dawn and yellow eyes flicker.
Where are my dogs? Growling in sleep.

Back in the morning, the dogs
tear apart their beloved toy. Poor man,
I tell them, little thing is dead.
I try to put the stuffing back.
I've fed them their kibble, their bit of meat.
They eye me at my desk, bent over blank paper.

We go out in the fog the morning won't burn.
The dogs go wild with sniffing.
Noses down, they pace in circles
where something existed,
panting on the road
where they last glimpsed him.
They can wait all day.
Hush, hush, I coax: he's long gone.

5.

Winter passes: dogs on the floor,
their dream-whimpers, their licks.
The crippled old one
pricks his ears and whines.
He'd been a wolf, loping through woods.
He looks at you, and transformation
is what you should have seen. Old dog, old dog,
drop the disguise, and run.

6.

What you say to the dog: no dying tonight!
Too soon, too cold, and his beloved snow
has come, a thick coat
glazing lashes and lids, the little pile of it
sitting on his nose. Black nose quivering,
held up for the fall. Turn your back
and he's pushing past the fence, the drifting
thigh-high, the white grave of it:
what *is* it he sees swaddled in white?
And now the snow's biting,
bits so little they make a strobe in the air's
slanted theater, blind home,
where the dog wants to go.

Stop whining, here's a cookie!
White hair, white light, a sigh of relenting
when he lets himself down.
One hip shudders, the other falls. Can this be pain
when the bed's so soft, hindquarters cushioned.
Too much saintliness
will wear us all down.
Mouth kisses everywhere
even from the terrier, and the cats
come close with their sniffing regard.
The dog is made of heaven, dog's life chugs on.
His *going-on*, his *now*, needing to be
brought to a halt—and you not able to see
his eyes full of you
done with and gone.

7.

Daily the ruined rise out of snow.
The terrier spends hours dragging forth
whatever she uncovers, not clean bones
but dank, fur-covered—hooves still attached.

The snow is tending toward nothingness,
frozen water whose melting
goes jagged and sheer on the path.
And when you fail to feed the birds,
the finches go elsewhere, living without as they do.
The blameless reappear, that small scrambling.

So much springs back—
silence sweeps through, a voice in its breath:
Fearful one, when were you not beloved?

8.

I'm drawn by the creaking—
time to bring the dead limbs down! A forked one
cracks, braced by a bough right over my head.
I screech, the little dog leaps—
oh the chugging engine of her heart,
tongue hanging out, red petal.
More, the terrier pants, all her dumb self quivering,
rolling, four legs swimming in the sunny air.
Clown dog, somersault queen of sticks.
This, it occurs to me, is funny—here I am,

lost in dog. I regard the big one
lying there, savoring in his masked way,
white angel ruffling. I look where he looks:
eyeing the wind in simple green, a spider of color
dotting the boughs. The black made more visible,
the dead more dead.

9.

How will you do it all without him,
he asks with his eyes, steady as always
on your every shudder, the tremulous rise in your voice.
Any sign of dismay obliges him
to lay his head in your lap.

So when his body, bullied into change,
pushes him to fall down sideways,
his brain slipping its curiosity aside,
eyes and ears falling second to intuition,
and even danger seems an indifferent thing,
he will try to go to the woods, or any hidden place,
as if to an origin some instinct
has handed down, centuries
before the human generations of home.

When your back is turned,
he'll go find a rock, a fallen tree,
a clump of hemlock where he'll just lie down.
His dignity in the last breath brought on by night's cold,
or something strong and hungry, not malevolent—

this is what the dog wants.
The worst thing would be to frighten you.

10.

On the day he died, I went out to hit trees.
It had been a long winter with unforgiving winds,
too cold for snow, and the woods were knotted
with fallen limbs caught high above ground.
I swung with a stick, thrashing over my head
till the dead parts flew, cracking or flying back.
Some trees were broken off, jagged
around the heartwood, that dense central core.
I fought deeper in, careless
with branches three or four time my length, thicker
than my arm. I had to balance and dodge,
practiced in the art of stumbling.
The burden rained down.
It was hard work and my palms bled,
and on the backs of my hands, the slammed skin,
the punished veins rising mottled and blue.
But it was good, freeing up the newly green,
even if hopeless in those woods—the forest floor
tired and littered with the winter kill.

11.

In the animal crematorium you wait
and wait—he is a big dog

and the business of burning
is long, and his long dying day
means the night is long, because the life
he lived is long, and there is nothing to do
but pick and pick at the long white hair
covering your coat, adding it to the fistful
you cut before they took him.
A bouquet of hair you cling to,
along with the blanket deep with his smell,
and the worn collar too, the tags
that list his name with yours
biting into your palm.

The room is small, an afterthought
to harbor the waiting—the tea things, the photos
of other beloveds lining the walls.
Airtight, nothing to interrupt
the fire boiling on the other side
of the concrete holding wall,
devouring the material: a maelstrom
of spit and belly and bone
that will forever keep away
unthinkable rot—

And now they come finally
with the grit and stone,
the *essence* they call it, this residue

poured in a box—with white roses
to adorn the box, for the taking away
of something so very light.
None of the heft we arranged on the table, so much

like a dog asleep on his side—
how can this be: white dog, white box,
and the crossing in flames.
You are deaf with the roar, you a burned boat
bearing a stone box bearing
ashes still hot in your hands,
and you carry it with you, unbroken seal.

12.

Three days of packing and the little one has given up.
No more sad-eyed contact- pleading
look-at-me; no following
from room to room, shadowing
each move from bureau to box.
No leash at the door, no collar, no sign
she's going in the car, or that someone, anyone
might come take this stuff away, leaving them
in the house where they belong—

Underfoot, she's acted out
the question, begging,
keeping herself in the way.
But now that the bed's been stripped,
she turns, leaves for another room,
pretends to hear nothing
as she finds her tossed blanket, turns round
to wrap herself, and lies down
facing the corner, the wall, fixed

on the blank, bottom space
where nothing can happen.

13.

On the cape, in the changing season,
under that noise

of sloshing against pilings, the push-in-
push-away, close then farther out;

underneath the gulls' bark, the desolate
ambient sound the dog understands—

the moving unstoppable current,
every complication reduced to repetition

as if to beat in some kind of lesson:
not urgency

in the water's fist
clenching and releasing, but *being*—

without need or purpose, and in my body all this time
the answering sweep of valves

opening and closing; just as the little
terrier, brimful of nerve and trembling,

alone, perched there, sentinel on the deck's edge,
has been trying all along to teach.

SALT WATER DUCKS

The tide ignores its limits, all last night
climbing over the railing, battering the door.
White spume flew its ghost against the glass.
The bay's in its third day of outrage,
but the ducks have to eat. The white-winged scoter
keeps me at the window, three sleek ones.
I count the in and out of their pristine heads—
bodies down for improbable minutes
before coming back up, black and white
against the white-capped black water shoving
against the row of stone pilings that mark the tide's high rise.
By eight a.m. I've seen enough
as the rocks submerge and the overwrought current,
something like a boxer pounding and pounding,
slams the ducks diving there—I've seen enough

to know what I'll find tomorrow on the wasted beach:
a washed-up duck, still intact,
limp sack beneath the flawless design
of its feathers, nothing odd except the crumpled pose.
Audubon propped them up on wires, a scaffold of bird—
no other way to capture life than to show it dead.
Brutality's not part of art's equation, we like to think.
Meanwhile, the birds are all instinct
in the moment. This life in a wild wind
is only the din they live in. I doubt they even hear it.

DUNE SHACK

To live in this place, you have to kill things.
At first you think you'll wait, you're innocent, the one
no one can blame. All those fixed
notions of what you could count on: the old life
made it possible to look the other way. But out here,
you have to deal with the obvious.
The maimed, the hopeless—
they're all around, they're waiting. Otherwise,
would your eye twitch, your right leg shake?

By the third day you've scoured the place,
but hunger being what it is, the mother mouse
moves right in, deposits her half-inch
offspring in some cotton you left unguarded.
And hearing her scratch through the night
is made worse only by her disappearance—
who knows what marsh hawk got her
or some other closer beast
foraging around the stilted shack?

So: since you're who's left, who's responsible,
Number 1, get the little things out of hiding.
Number 2, just get it over with.

ALONE

The spider's long legs
more than mother
the glistening three-tiered web.
Tearing it only brings her back
resolved again, and patient—but oh
this deliberate dismantling, this person
waving a hand through it, shoving
the broken threads to the side,
brushing strands away from my face,
cursing how something still sticks
and clings, so I can't be done with it.

As if it were a plot, not a home
built with her very self. And this hunger—
this need to take all she can harvest
inside her, no end to her want—
no, how she keeps alive
is not luminous, but strict and necessary,
this moving sideways into the dark.

WESTERN CONIFER SEED BUG

He'd become a houseguest, noncommittal
and impassive. She tried to see to it
he wasn't disturbed, nothing to trip him up:
a book, perhaps, laid down
in some rash motion might scare him
off an edge, although he had a talent, it seemed,
for focusing on himself. He'd been so carefully
attended, she thought—warning her
guests to watch for him on the coverlet,
not overreact to his homely presence.
She kept close guard, as was her nature,
a kind of partner to help him make it
through the winter. She'd done the research
when he showed up; she knew all his business,
she had a duty. With these advantages,
how had he taken it upon himself to die?
But there he was in that trite pose,
feet in the air, as if arranged on the sink top
for her to find him. She brushed her teeth, considering
all the pine trees surrounding the house,
their heavy scent calling the half-sleeping one
at the rightful time. They were almost there—
he would have been free,
piercing and sucking that sap deep in the cones.

SURVIVAL: A GUIDE

It's not easy living here, waiting to be charmed
by the first little scribble of green. Even in May
crows want to own the place, and the heron, old bent thing,
spends hours looking like graying bark,
part of a dead trunk lying over opaque water.
She strikes the pose so long I begin to think
she's determined to make herself into something ordinary.
The small lakes continue their slide into bog and muck—
remember when they ran clear, an invisible spring
renewing the water? But the ducks stay longer, amusing
ruffle and chatter. I can be distracted.

If I do catch her move, the heron appears
to have no particular fear or hunger, her gaunt body
hinged haphazardly, a few gears unlocking
one wing, then another. More than a generation here
and every year more drab.
Once I called her blue heron, as in Great Blue,
true to a book—part myth, part childhood's color.
Older now, I see her plain: a mere surviving
against a weedy bank with fox dens
and the ruthless, overhead patrol.
Some blind clockwork keeps her going.

ACKNOWLEDGMENTS

Thanks to the following journals that published some of these new poems, often in different versions: *The Cortland Review*, *The Georgia Review*, *Ploughshares*, *The Southern Review*, *Sou'wester*, *The Threepenny Review*.

My utmost gratitude to the Guggenheim Foundation for their fellowship in support of this work. I am also grateful to the Corporation of Yaddo for residencies that allowed me the time and space I needed for these poems. For their loyal friendship and poetic support over many years, I want to thank Maudelle Driskell, Zack Finch, Louise Hamlin, Pamela Harrison, Cynthia Huntington, Gary Lenhart, Bill Mathis, Stanley Moss, Ann Phillips, Bill Phillips, Sara Warner Phillips, Stephen Phillips, Martha Rhodes, Stephanie Wolff, and especially Ellen Bryant Voigt, whose acute, loving vision sustains me, and Allison Funk for her invaluable help with this manuscript. With all my thanks to the Sarabande staff for their careful attention to my work, particularly Sarah Gorham and Jeffrey Skinner. To my children: Alexandra, Zachary, Simon, and Tessa, you are an abiding source of inspiration and support.

And with my love to Don Metz.

NOTES

"The River" is for Janine Kanzler, in memory of Jamie Kanzler, 1989–2013.

"As if mad is a direction, like west" is taken from the novel *Alias Grace* by Margaret Atwood.

CLEOPATRA MATHIS was born and raised in Ruston, Louisiana, and has lived in New England since 1980. She has published seven previous books of poems, most recently *Book of Dog* and *White Sea*, both from Sarabande Books. Her many awards and prizes include a Guggenheim Fellowship, two fellowships from the National Endowment for the Arts, and two Pushcart Prizes. Her poems have appeared widely in journals, magazines, and anthologies, including *The New Yorker*, *Threepenny Review*, *The Georgia Review*, *Best American Poetry*, and *The Extraordinary Tide: Poetry by American Women*. The founder of the creative writing program at Dartmouth College in 1982, she lives with her family in East Thetford, Vermont.

SARABANDE BOOKS is a nonprofit literary press located in Louisville, KY. Founded in 1994 to champion poetry, short fiction, and essay, we are committed to creating lasting editions that honor exceptional writing. For more information, please visit sarabandebooks.org.